THROUGH THE
STORM

Helping Marriages find
Healing after Hurt

Emily Rose Funderburk, LPC

WESTBOW
PRESS®
A DIVISION OF THOMAS NELSON
& ZONDERVAN

THE HOLY BIBLE, NEW INTERNATIONAL VERSION®,
NIV® Copyright © 1973, 1978, 1984, 2011 by Biblica, Inc.®
Used by permission. All rights reserved worldwide.

WestBow Press books may be ordered through booksellers or by contacting:

WestBow Press
A Division of Thomas Nelson & Zondervan
1663 Liberty Drive
Bloomington, IN 47403
www.westbowpress.com
1 (866) 928-1240

Because of the dynamic nature of the Internet, any web addresses or
links contained in this book may have changed since publication and
may no longer be valid. The views expressed in this work are solely those
of the author and do not necessarily reflect the views of the publisher,
and the publisher hereby disclaims any responsibility for them.

Any people depicted in stock imagery provided by Getty Images are
models, and such images are being used for illustrative purposes only.
Certain stock imagery © Getty Images.

ISBN: 978-1-9736-4692-1 (sc)
ISBN: 978-1-9736-4694-5 (hc)
ISBN: 978-1-9736-4693-8 (e)

Library of Congress Control Number: 2018914087

Print information available on the last page.

WestBow Press rev. date: 12/14/2018

Contents

*For Matthew, thank you for weathering every storm
with me, embracing every sunrise by my side, and seeing
the rainbows when all I see are clouds. You are the gift
I don't deserve. Can I keep you forever? 1437*

*For Aidan, Noah, and Rosalee, I know you didn't fully understand
why I spent hours in front of a computer, and you questioned if I
was actually writing a book. Here it is. I know I owe you a lot of
homecooked meals and family game-nights, but one day I hope you see
this was why, and because helping people find freedom will always be
important to your Dad and I. You three will never know how much
you have taught me and I can't wait to read all the stories you write.
May the weather outside never determine how you see the world. <3*

*For you, the couple that is hurting. This was crafted, cried over,
and battled through so you wouldn't feel alone and so you would
find hope in a world that is trying to steal it. You are stronger
than you know, and you're about to have your own story to tell.*

*For the church, I wrote you a letter to open this book,
because we have to love the hurting, we have to get
this part right. Thank you for leaning in.*

A Letter to the Church Before We Get Started

Church,

Some couples walk through your doors that will sit closer to each other on Sunday than any other day of the week. Couples that are hurting, couples that are desperate, couples planning their exit strategy, and couples hiding behind a mask of shame with the situation they are in. We need to love these people. We need to be safe places for people to feel ashamed because we have the antidote for this cancer. We need to welcome vulnerability, but also care for the people that have opened up to us. Couples in a storm shouldn't be treated like they have leprosy – hug them, approach them, bring them dinner, and babysit their kids.

Leaders in the church, your community doesn't know how to do this; you have to teach them. We have to teach people how to love the hurting.

Fellow brothers and sisters, you're going to get pushback, people are going to leave your church because of the way you love the broken, but we must. You have to model grace; you have to protect vulnerable stories, you have to lean into the people that the elders would advise you to keep your distance from, and financially support the couples who don't know how to get help for themselves. Care for them, and love the people that feel like they don't deserve your love. Let's do more than talk about Jesus, let's be the hands and feet and infect light in every crevice that the darkness tries to reach. Let's lead proclaiming the good news in how we treat others. Let us be the church that shows GRACE to its people and not just talk about it when it fits in with our sermon.

My last urge to you, the couples that are hurting the most aren't always the ones that sit in your pews. Some of the most devastating stories are happening right around your Monday morning staff team. The church staff team that feels like they aren't allowed to talk about their brokenness. The Children's Director whose husband is battling pornography and she has lost a sense of her self-worth. The Campus Pastor who crossed the line with a married woman last week and is too afraid to get counsel on his regrets. Even the Lead Pastor, who has neglected his wife after giving every bit of himself into the church. The people around the leadership table are not immune from struggles, care for them in the middle of their storms. Public shaming has become our reputation in dealing with private sin. The community is watching. They are seeing your public denouncement of your past staff member, but not seeing you love them. How we treat regrets and mistakes will teach our congregation how we truly feel about grace, compassion, and shame. We can't preach on Sunday about forgiveness, and that healing is to be found in the name of Jesus, when we tell our staff in their storms: "good luck and hopefully you can find healing somewhere other than here." We teach love by showing love. We teach hope by believing in people even when they are on their worst day. The most significant sermons you give won't happen on Sunday; they will happen in the way you care for your team and their families.

Love one another. Be the church with your staff team. Check on your staffs' spouses. Let's love the hurting and give people undeserved compassion that the world will think is unfair. The Church should turn heads by the way we love the underserved, not in the way we look like every other business on the street.

Just love, friend. Love the sinners. Love the mistake-makers (remembering that you are one). Love the addicts. Love the stealers. Love the unjust. Love the abused and victimized. Just love. Stop making your appearance matter more than the way you love others.

Thank you for listening, thank you for being an example in the way you love one another and thank you for providing beacons of hope for the hopeless relationships and situations. If they can't walk through your doors, where else will they go?

Emily

Step I
BREATHE

You know that thing your body does instinctually every day without you ever giving it a second thought, we're gonna start with that. Take a breath for a moment and just focus on your breathing. But this time, as you breathe, remind yourself you're breathing. Let's do it together. Take a deep inhale through your nose, follow the air with your mind as it flows down through your throat and now feel it fill up your lungs. Now take one, big, long, exhale, as you release the air, drop your shoulders, and continue to just breathe.

Sit at the Same Table

These pages are filled for the broken-hearted, for the confused, for the off-course, for the spouses that feel like saints, and the spouses that have been reminded they are sinners. These pages are filled with moments of crisis and the scrambling of bringing order to the existing chaos in your home that you may be living in right now. These pages are the same no matter which house reads them, but the hands that hold these pages each have a different story to tell. What remains the same is the common reality of surviving a storm, but first, is the reminder to breathe. This journey is a course in breathing through a crisis, of stopping and learning how to see through the fog your marriage feels like it is in here at this moment.

This is not a self-help-want-a-better-marriage book; there are plenty of those you can read. This is an I'm-not-sure-what-to-do-next-and-this-marriage-feels-hopeless book. That's why you're here, and you are not alone, we're all sitting at the same table.

We are all sitting at the same table

Even though I'm not sure what the storm of your marriage/family looks like right now, I can take a guess. It might consist of words that are attacking instead of uplifting. It might be filled with an atmosphere of condemnation. It might be filled with friends and family that are angry and voices directed at shame and judgment. It might even be filled with an intense quiet and avoidance of everything that is going on. Whatever your world is filled with, these pages are your moments of peace among attacks and criticisms and uncertainty. There is no judgment here, you both have enough of that in your life already. This book is your place to breathe and a place where we will all talk like we are sitting at the same table. Here's what I mean:

It's easy to judge people when we aren't all sitting at the same table. Any time shame creates a hierarchy we distance people from one another, and the same thing can happen in your home. One spouse could be kneeling on the floor feeling unworthy to sit at the table, or one spouse could have moved a pedestal over to the table to sit higher in their entitlement. You're here because you want to know what to do next, so for starters, let's make our first step to take a breath and invite all our marriages to come and sit at the same table.

We've got some tough stuff we're going to lay out and talk through. Sin isn't a pretty thing to deal with, and it can even feel taboo to talk about in most circles. We're getting it out, and we're going to let the light penetrate the dark areas of our personal lives while asking God to do the impossible and heal what seems like the unredeemable areas in our marriages.

First, we have to sit at the table together as we talk about the storms swirling overhead. We can pull up a chair and sit at the same table by acknowledging that we all go through storms and in recognizing that we all have an authentic story right alongside them. We breathe by linking our authenticity with our humility in sitting at the table together. No one is higher right now than the other, and no one has fallen from grace further than the other. That's how we start at the table together.

Without the experience of going through someone else's storm, you can't judge or know what someone is going through in their life. At the same table, we listen to experiences, and we are present in someone else's story. Don't assume you understand someone else, even that person that you committed your life to. Instead, let's open our eyes and ears at the table together and see the beating hearts that are beside us. If we can't understand a tsunami until we hear someone give their devastating experience of it, then let's sit at the table and hear their experience before we blame them for not having flood insurance.

Everyone has an authentic story

Our cloudiest days and our sunniest moments are filled with the authenticity of our personal stories. So here we are, this is your invitation to join us at the table, and whether your spouse comes too, only time will tell, but they are invited right alongside you at the table.

As you unfold your story, know you are safe here. No page is going to tell you that you are worthless. No page will treat you like a piece of dirt on the floor, in fact, we'll talk about how to see something wholly made new. Know you are safe to feel here too. You are safe here to be angry, safe to be scared, safe to be unsure, and safe to feel hopeless. You are safe to feel here, but I hope you won't stay in that sadness but that we learn how to find love, joy, peace, patience, kindness, goodness, faithfulness, gentleness, and self-control (Galatians 5:22) through the storm you are in. That is the hope for what is ahead.

There is authenticity in the storm stories of your life and your marriage. Without walking in your shoes, or you stepping foot in mine, we must respect the stories we don't understand. As we journey together through the storm in our marriages, our vulnerability with each other will come alongside the safety of respect for where your marriage is at today, and being and doing the best you feel able to do on this one day.

As you think about your storm, it may be similar or different to the other storm stories ahead. No matter the story, there are valuable lessons, practical steps, and God-honoring truth that can unite the way we deal with the aftermath of a storms existence in your life and the life of your marriage. We'll go through exercises that will challenge you, encouragement that will crack lights of hope in the darkest corners, and truth statements that will redefine the way we talk about love and forgiveness. Those are glimpses at what's ahead, but first, let's all start by taking a breath and sitting at the same table.

Jesus is at the table

Jesus is at the table too. He was the first to show us that we need to sit together. He reminds us that we sit at the table together because we all have worth. You have a worth you can't even fathom in the eyes of the God that loves you. Truly. Loves. You. He has the answer to the WebMD questions you are asking right now about your worth, your value, and your hope.

Jesus shows us a new way to handle the people that were deemed worthless, sinners, and the hopeless situations. People may cast you aside, a family member may be treating you or your marriage like it has lost its worth, but Jesus models something different, and I believe we can apply those truths in the upcoming pages to your marriage as well.

Jesus was sitting with the people that everyone thought not to associate with, the people and the relationships that were considered a lost cause, he sat with them at the same table. Jesus was seen with the unclean, the dirty, and the people that didn't call themselves clean but needed to be cleaned. During that time, Jesus got a lot of attention for just sitting at the same table with these outcasts. People questioned his motives, but then came his response, "It is not the healthy who need a doctor, but the sick. I have not come to call the righteous, but sinners" (Mark 2:17; Luke 5:31; and Matt 9:12).

This same statement applies to you as a person. You. Wherever you are right now, whatever you have done, whatever worth and hope seems lost in the relationships of your life, we are going to sit at the same table as we discover some great news: Jesus came for the sick and the broken, and this applies to your marriage as well. Jesus knows that our unhealthy, fallen nature and sin-filled desires are residing in our hearts and has a significant influence on our marriages and families. You turned here because you feel sick, your marriage has hit the bottom of a pit, and you need a doctor. There is a prescription.

We are going to turn to our Doctor who has the answers we are looking for. The Father that provides healing in restoring our soul through the grueling but necessary process of recovery while giving us hope at repairing the damage these storms have inflicted in both us and our marriage. It's going to take work, but even more, it's going to bring growth.

Every storm can have a story of overcoming connected to it, but overcoming takes growth. You are about to grow, whether you like it or not because the road ahead is going to be hard, but worth it. If you were my six-year-old, I would get prepared to take you to the shoe store because you are about to go through a growth spurt, the both of you. People will recognize the difference, so let's make it one worth recognizing. Let's find the rainbow through this nasty storm. You have support, and you aren't alone. Even on the loneliest days, you aren't alone. Let's use this storm as an opportunity for victory instead of a struggle to insanity. Here we go.

From me to you

It is with a reverent and hopeful heart that these pages have been crafted. Throughout this book, you will see the blend of my experience as a professional counselor helping other couples, my studies and practice of God's word, and most importantly the work that God has first done in myself and my marriage to get us through the most glorious and ugliest of days. Throughout the book, you will see small exerts that I took directly out of my personal journal during times in my life where I felt my God, and my journal were all I had to cling to.

Chapter 1
Brace for Impact

This morning's weather forecast brought the news that a hurricane watch is underway in our area. For our city, a storm scare like this means that by the end of the day, word will have spread about the forecast and every person with a smartphone will be checking the radar maps and becoming social media friends with our local meteorologists. In our area, we won't be able to end the day without filling up our vehicles with gas and purchasing gallons of milk and loaves of bread to survive whatever is headed our way. I'm not sure where we'll be going, or if the vehicle will be able to hold all the milk and bread we are about to buy, but we all will scatter around the city trying to do something about something we can't do anything about.

A hurricane watch could mean anything and nothing all at once. We could get a soft wind gust, harsh rains, collapsed trees, or roofs blown off the houses in our neighborhood. It is predictably unpredictable. The experts give us educated guesses, but we just don't know what is coming until it gets here.

We all stare at our television screens waiting to see what amount of force this storm will bring once it hits land.

There is fear everywhere.

Anticipation fills the streets as we wonder what direction these gusts are headed, and whether we will get a tropical storm or a bit of rain, or if this will be the big news story people talk about for years to come.

There is panic.
There is worry.
There is fear.

Everyone is bracing for impact. No one feels safe, and the security of stocked pantries and gas-fueled cars bring a sense of control to a situation that is entirely out of our control.

When a storm is coming, worry wells up as something way bigger than any one person is headed our way. We brace for impact with the unsettling emotions of the unknown, the limitless possibilities of what could happen, and what kind of influence this will have on tomorrow.

Yesterday seemed so normal, but today, everyone is worried about how to survive without the basic comforts of electricity in their homes, gas to fuel their cars, and food to stock their pantries.

In a world full of planners, there are some things we just can't fully predict, and the weather is one of them. We may try and guess what's coming, but fully predicting the weather just isn't possible. When a storm happens, it will feel unavoidable, and once it is here, we have to weather the storm. We can't ignore the weather. And as the people in our city stay hidden behind their closed doors waiting to see what happens, I can't help but compare how our reactions and responses to the storms occurring outside our homes look similar to the ones raging on inside of them.

As our city braces for impact today for the physical storm on the horizon, my thoughts are filled with the houses that had their major emotional storms hit last week. I think of the inside of homes all around me that are active right now in a storm of hurt, a storm of sadness, quiet storms of isolation, hidden storms of secrecy, and so many more. They are happening. There are marriages and families all over wishing their current storms would just pass.

They feel stuck.
They feel hopeless.
They feel scared.

With whatever is going on outside in our community, I want to bring a forecast into the people glued to these pages, hoping for some good news with the storm they are in.

Without warning, without even hesitation, there can be real-life torrential storms whose relational wind gusts come in and effect all the personal areas of your home. With no forecast, no evacuation notice, and not even an alert reminder on your phone of what is headed your way, your whole world can feel like it is crashing down when a storm enters the comfort of your home.

Today that might be you. Your household is hurting. Your family is bruised, and your marriage is questioning what to do next. If you're in the middle of panic, struggling to get out of the dark clouds around you, and feeling lost while standing in front of the person who used to be your best friend, these pages are for you. A storm may have swept in, but we aren't going to let it overtake you. Not today.

Sin Storms

When we brace for impact, we get prepared for a storm, all the while not sure what is coming until it gets here. In the lives of our families, there will be many storms that we all will endure. So many couples and families have been through all sorts of storms, and just as Mother Nature gives us different types of storms (hurricanes, earthquakes, tsunamis, etc..), there are a few different types of situational storms that will test and try your marriage. I wonder if your premarital counselor gave you the warning that your marriage would go through tragedy storms, transitional storms, and sin storms.

Tragedy storms come unexpectedly in the night with no explanation, such as a sudden illness, a significant job loss, or a devastating weather event that threatens your livelihood. Tragedy storms are unplanned events that put your whole life into upheaval. When it's supposed to be easy to get pregnant, and we learn with devastation that this is going to be a long road, - we go through tragedy together as a couple. As a doctor gives news of a life-threatening illness, we go through a tragedy storm. These heartrending seasons will shake and rattle our worlds and change our perspectives on everything around us. Life becomes tough, and every day going through a tragedy storm will feel like a battle.

Transitional storms are seasons in your life when dynamic shifts occur and cause the family system to realign and adjust to a new normal. Job and moving transfers can create all sorts of new seasons for the family. Even a new addition like adding a baby to the mix creates a storm that has both blessing and trial all in the same package. Empty nesters go through the transitional storm of letting go and learning to cling to their spouses once again. These transitions test and try us to learn to adapt and grow with each new circumstance we go through as a couple.

Sin storms are my term for the havoc that is created when the weaknesses and struggles in our lives get magnified in our marriage and families. Sin storms enter our home when one or both spouses engage in sinful desires and allow something to come before their Creator and their spouse.

Storms can sweep through our lives just like the thunderstorm that wakes you up from a peaceful sleep. You may have had a warning, or you could have never seen this coming. Sin storm stories are all around us. Stories of storms that your friends, family, and even your own household have been through. Storms of sexual immorality, a pornography struggle, substance abuse addiction, hurtful anger, gambling, emotional or physical abuse, neglect, or any other form of unfaithfulness that surfaces in the home. When you go through a sin storm, the walls that were built for protection will become filled with rain clouds. Immediately, the hurt and hate you feel will bring winds into the house that could knock you both over. Within an instant, everything will feel like you are living in a dream.

Sin storms will create an experience in your home that will leave all family members feeling like they are swirling in some sort of tornado. When you are the spouse who has something to hide, exposed shame will hit your fantasy world like a ton of bricks. You begin to see your web of lies and now feel stuck in a mess you've created. When you are the spouse who is shocked with decisions made right under your nose, your world feels like it no longer makes sense and your sense of security feels like it just flew out the window with the storm.

All this chaos disrupts the very foundation of your home. You both feel like Dorothy in The Wizard of Oz being taken off to a distant land while longing and clicking your heels to just get back home. Your home. The home that as you both unpacked boxes you were declaring was your safe place from a scary world. But when these sin storms happen in your home, it doesn't matter if there was a forecast warning or not. You will both feel crushed, and home won't feel as safe anymore.

We have all gone through storms. We might give varying definitions on what a category 2 versus a category 5 hurricane may look like in our house, but most of us have felt one, and know too well the scary reality of walking through and standing next to an unpredictable storm.

Marital Storms

Wherever you are today, whatever area you live in, and whatever season you are going through, one thing we have in common is that we share the same weather forecast. It just hits at different points in our lives, and the impact may look different in yours than it does in mine.

For the sake of these pages, and for the place you are at right now in your life, we are going to focus on the storms related to your marital relationship. You may be bracing for impact, buying the store out of milk and bread so that you can make it through the marital storm you are in.

The marriage you are sitting in right now that may contain

tornadoes of yelling. The marital storm that has you questioning whether you both should just evacuate. The marital lightning-bolts of lying, swarms of secrets, infidelity, abuse, isolation, and addiction, are shaking the foundation of everything you once thought was stable and secure.

You are in a storm, and you know you can't live like this any longer.

So much is happening, so much that you are almost speechless, feeling formless, and unable to think without clarity. These storms are consuming, suffocating, and emotionally heartbreaking to the fiber of your being.

We all have a Storm Story

I talk about storms with familiarity because I have the scars of walking through them and my husband and I have the story of strength and hope of persevering through some of the scariest circumstances we wouldn't wish anyone had to experience. But others do, I have heard their stories. I have listened to the heartbreaking stories of the pieces people don't like to talk about. There is so much sadness, but I see hope and strength in every crevice that sadness attempts to surface. The stories I hear of people opening up with a courageous vulnerability show me that every person has a story much like each finger has a unique print, and every storm has a unique effect.

A sin storm can tear your personal world apart, and with greater influence is the effects your sinful decisions will have on the life of your entire family. In a marriage, we see the beauty of blending two people together, but when a storm enters that marriage, it aims to destroy what was meant to be brought together.

As we go forward, we will uncover how to walk through a marital storm, how to survive the darkest days where you see no end in the marriage that presently feels hopeless, and how to look in the mirror again and see someone that has value. We will uncover the reality of a tomorrow that seems impossible to even fathom at this point. There is a tomorrow coming, this storm will have an end, and with intentionality, there will be a purpose to this storm as it turns into a part of your story instead of the identity of your life.

I know you both might not be there yet. You could be feeling like this is your life, this is your identity, and this is now the label your life will carry on the front of your shirt. You may even feel worthless, and you could be debating whether the future of this marriage is a lost cause. Friend, your feelings aren't always your reality, but I get that the voice that wants to rob you from freedom wants that perception to be true. It's time to uncover the truth and find it from the only source that gives our lives and our marriages the healing it so desperately needs right now.

Time for the Forecast

Today, as our city plans for the days to come, we are surrounded by rain and wet and cold outside. Something is happening, the rain is but a taste of the harsh winds behind it. As we stare at our television screens for predictions, we find comfort and anxiety in seeing what is ahead. A bit of sun on Tuesday, harsh winds on Wednesday, rain on Thursday, and a beautiful forecast for Friday. Here's the point: there is a future. There is a forecast beyond today. Beyond the days on the screen that say torrential, there are still more days to come. The seven-day forecast fills us with the days of worry and days of hope with the reminder that there is an AFTER this storm.

If the weather forecast gives us eyes into tomorrow, it's time to provide you with your forecast. For your life, for wherever your marriage is, as we get started, I want to give you a forecast right now. I know the clouds are dark. I know your tears match the rain, and you have moments where you've forgotten what the sun feels like on your face, but the future is bright. It doesn't feel like that I know, but this is where we find our forecast in the truth of God's light, and in the Creator that holds the universe in His hands.

We know the future includes the sun because the sun doesn't leave because a storm enters our life. The sun doesn't leave its place in the universe, and its brightness doesn't waver, the only thing that changes with the sun is what we see of it. You might not see much when you look at your marriage and think through the storms you are going through. You may not feel this truth today, on this rainy day filled with panic, but whether you feel it today or not, there is a sun that is shining and it is shining right where you are at. We are going to walk through the days of this storm together and find the other side of it as we see past the rain. Brace for impact, there is so much ahead.

Chapter 2
Seeing our Sinful Nature

Being "that couple"

My authenticity begins with unashamedly admitting that I don't have the perfect marriage. (Wait…did you not want to hear that from the author of this book? I guess we are practicing how to appreciate authenticity

Journal: I can't see past the struggle, I can't see past the pain of today and the weight of shame that feels like a noose around my neck has made itself a home and feels as though it won't ever let go.

right here, right now.) The beginning stages for us was a hope for smooth sailing and an illusion that we were immune to anything interfering into the beauty of "us." As a Counselor, I have always been passionate about helping other couples, but in our home, we were never supposed to be "that couple."

You know "that couple" that everyone looks at and says, "at least we aren't like them," or "we might have problems, but at least they don't look like 'that couple.'"

Our marriage has gone through seasons that left us feeling isolated from one another, hurting each other, and left us questioning whether there was anything left to fight for. We have had long stretches of feeling whole and beautiful, and we have also had seasons of feeling disgraced and broken. We have learned that "to be alive is to be broken" (Manning, 1990).

Early on, our young hearts didn't understand what to do with the storms that we had to endure and how God was going to use them to strengthen our marriage. I can personally look back at my life now and see that I had hoped to be an exception to the rule as I teach others the rules. Walking with the Lord in the desert, and falling to your knees in humility will do a number to your soul. I believe the Lord walks with us, comforts us, and guides us in the storms because He sees something in our marriages that we don't see at times; I believe He even sees things in me that I don't see at times.

When we get married, we never believe we are going to be "that couple" that goes through "that struggle," whatever "that" happens to be for you. If you are reading this book now, it's because you are there, and you are desperate. My guess is you won't put it down because you don't know what to do next. You might not have even realized there was a next, and you aren't getting the answers to the specific questions you have been googling.

All storms are difficult to go through, the expected and the unexpected, and the invited and the uninvited. The invited and uninvited sin storms are where we get the most stuck. When the ripple effects to the consequences of sin are most evident, and the potential for ripple storms to come on the horizon are at their peak. Sin storms aim at complete and entire destruction that leaves us not knowing what just happened and confused about what to do next with many families quickly believing there isn't even going to be a next.

When we are married, and a storm of sin enters our personal lives we have to face the fact that the solution is not just a personal problem. Every decision we make impacts and influences our marriages and families. The storms in our personal lives will create storms in every area our life touches. They are all connected, they all reside in the same town and suffer the same weather forecast.

My marriage is filled with the greatest days I wish I could relive over and over, but also days with unanticipated storms, and storms that one or both of us could have prevented. We have both been loved by each other, and both hurt by each other as well. We've had to learn how to love each other through the storms we thought would break us, and the storms we didn't even see coming. Our storm stories have taught us how to love each other intensely through the storms we never want to re-encounter.

We have been "that couple," and we have spent time judging "those couples" as well. Judging taught us nothing that strengthened ourselves, but being "that couple" humbled us completely. Whatever storm you are in, whatever storms you have been through, it is authentic to your story, but let's not miss the opportunity to all humble ourselves from the start of this journey and just admit right now that we are all "that couple." We are all at the same table.

Married to a Sinner

We get the opportunity to learn what it means to love someone by spending the rest of our lives, and our personal space with them. There is nowhere to hide in marriage, and this union brings with it the beauty of togetherness and the reminder that we are broken together as well. Easy to write now, but a grueling lesson to walk through and learn first-hand. We come face-to-face with Mother Nature every day we step outside, so it only makes sense that our Sinful Nature will surface itself in the inside of our homes.

There comes a season in our marriages when we realize that our prince charming is a sinner, and even more than that you realize that the sweet, kind-hearted princess is a sinner too. Seasons when our weaknesses surface. And learning to love in the middle of exposed weakness becomes a strength none of us feel equipped for. And when you see your perfect spouse's brokenness, it can be hard to see anything else. You both knew you were sinners, but never to the extent that you would do something to harm the person you committed your life to.

Each couple seems to have an authentic story of when they first recognized that the person they married wasn't the person they married. The intimate friendship they once shared just isn't the same, and the seasons in their marriage where us against the world turned into us against each other.

In our life, we came into our marriage knowing that we were both broken and flawed, but expecting to never be broken or flawed towards each other. We understood that "we all have sinned and fall short of the glory of God (Rom. 3:23)". I knew, and maybe you did too, that we married someone that was going to fall short in their obedience and faithfulness to God, but never, as newlyweds, did we understand that we would sin against our marriage and disobey our faithfulness to one another.

The extent of our sinful nature was supposed to be in the direction of our spiritual walk with God, not our spouse. That was the thought at least. We were only supposed to forgive each other for medial things like chores around the house and needing an attitude adjustment in the way we treat each other.

We all have a season where we learn the hard way, that in marriage, we see what it means to be broken together, two broken sinners. What you might not have seen were the swirling sin storms that blew into what seemed like the dead of night.

Our sin struggles don't stop once we get married, they only get magnified. Our struggles just get spotlighted because in marriage, someone is intertwined and a part of our life.

In any marriage, the storms of sexual immorality, a pornography struggle, addiction, anger, rage, abuse, neglect, and infidelity, just to name a few, can enter in when you both aren't careful and intentional to keep them out. Our marriage and the many marriages I have walked alongside have learned that you don't prepare for what you don't expect. Without intentionality, honesty, and obedience, we are all in for some trouble. Feeling above sin is the best way to be entrapped by a surprise attack. That's why we are all sitting here at the same table.

You may be right where we have been, these are lessons you know now, but now, it just feels too late. We came to a point in our marriage where we needed a step-by-step guideline on what to do next, and finding what to do next after a sin storm blows through has brought hope to many couples, and I know it can work for yours too.

We are ALL Unfaithful

You may not be ready to talk about hope just yet. I understand that. But hope is on the horizon. Hope is difficult right now mainly because it is a bit abnormal in our society. Our culture isn't even shocked anymore at our divorce statistic because the lack of hope after a storm surfaces in marriage has become normal. Divorce is almost considered justified once a sin is present. Not saying it's right, just saying that the real struggle in our society is that we don't know how to have hope after difficulties surface in marriage. Ending the marriage is the only resource many couples have been given. The first call after a crisis in your home may even be to a lawyer before you consider a counselor. The back door and a fresh start seem like the easiest option. But the easiest option isn't always the best one.

Let me tell you why I have hope. I believe that no matter how high the divorce rate gets, the statistic that isn't changing is the fact that we will all experience a 100% rate of unfaithfulness in our marriages.

You heard that right. We are all unfaithful. And since we are all unfaithful, we will all need persistent lessons in repentance.

If you didn't believe me say that we are all sitting at the same table, this is what I am talking about. We will all fall short in caring for one another just like we all fall short in our obedience to God. We all need a Savior, not only "that couple" that we used to judge, us all. We will all have moments where we struggle to love our spouses deeply, to care about them selflessly, and we all have seasons where we leave our spouse feeling forgotten and will turn to something in this world instead of our spouse. That can be food for you, obsession with social media, or even video games that are hard to turn off. The list of unfaithfulness is bigger than your judgments on what unfaithfulness is or looks like. We are all unfaithful.

Not your definition of unfaithful right? Well, that's what it means to be unfaithful to God, to put something of this world before Him. That can be an addiction of any kind (even the things you keep hidden that you don't even consider a problem in your life); any comfort or approval from another person that you rely on before God; the hope you get from the stability of your bank account; and even inappropriate images that distract you from the emotions you should be dealing with in your life.

God and the "unfaithful people" of Israel and Judah

Need an example? God even called the city of Israel and Judah an "unfaithful people" (Jer 3:6-18) because they were turning to something besides Him for their hope and salvation. They cheated on Him, over and over and over again. They were considered adulterers because of their conduct and neglect of God. This was true for them, and it happens in our life as well.

Israel turns away, but God doesn't leave them abandoned to their unfaithful decisions. He invites them back. He was angry, but He also said to them "I will not look on you with anger, for I am unfailing in my love" (Jeremiah 3:12).

I have hope for my marriage and hope for your marriage because I believe in the God that restores, reconciles, and heals all forms of adultery and addictions. The God that gives us examples in the Bible, and examples of couples walking all around us, that are coming together after turning to something else. A faithful God that doesn't let go of us even when we are faithfully disobedient to Him. We are all unfaithful, and that means that if the divorce statistic is 50% where you live, that means that 50% of people are staying together after unfaithfulness too. Every marriage tends to face some type of unfaithfulness. Whether it's something you consider big or small makes no difference in the world, it's all unfaithful and needs to be addressed.

So here you are, and I know this was never supposed to be you guys, we thought that about us too. You are in a storm. The storms of unfaithfulness, abuse, addiction, pornography, piles of lies, or something similar has entered into your marriage, and you don't know what to do with the shattered debris on the floor. The only options you see may be to clean up the dirt, walk away from the mess, or brush it under the rug and hope it never resurfaces. These all feel like your only options, but there is more.

We are faced with the reality of marriages that got off course through the storms of sin's destructive deceit and our conscious and unconscious decisions related to it. We are going to dissect our hearts and marriages with the strengths and weaknesses that currently lie within it. My warning to you is that if you are living in a marriage without broken people and with two entirely blameless spouses, you may not get much benefit from what comes next.

This book was written for "that couple" from the heart of "that couple". This book is for the broken. This book is designed with authentic stories in mind and for the marriages that don't look like the image they wanted, hoped for, or believed God wants their marriage to resemble. These pages will connect to people that wish for a sunny 7-day forecast but feel it is impossible to ever get to that. If that's not you, or if you are not aware yet that without intentionality and work this could be you, you will find yourself more critical and feeling above the storm clouds than relating to the real struggle of sin and the beauty that marriage brings to our life. Let's look outside, as we sit at the same table, and see something beautiful on its way from the horizon. There is hope to be found.

Hopeful Promises Beyond our Sinful Nature

For those of you that aren't getting a source of loving support and are only hearing voices of condemnation and slander, let this book serve as truth in your life, remembering that all the people around you are in shock and are hurt and need time to process what they are feeling.

Amidst the hurtful words you are hearing, know there are still promises that Jesus has claimed over you, promises to be seen in a new light, and promises that we won't fully be able to understand unless we do this restoration part right. Restoring the soul and cleansing the mind has to start with each of you, with admitting where you were not walking in line with the character of Christ, and believing that God can pick up the shattered pieces off the floor and put together something beautiful.

We don't have to look far to find the promises that God gives us to have hope in our lives and instruction with our sinful nature. Right now, no matter the blame of who did what, we first have to understand our sinful nature before we can argue about it. Glimpses of hope might be hard to accept once the ugliness of sin peaks its existence, but over time hope will become encrypted on your heart. A great example is found in the book of Romans.

No matter the fault in your marriage, you both can be encouraged by looking at sin, death, and finding new life in Christ through the powerful words Paul displays in Romans. We gain a better understanding of God's poetic nature in hearing that just as sin was brought into the world through one man, Adam, God's grace was shown to the world also through one man, Jesus Christ (Romans 5:15). Jesus is the answer for our hope. "For just as through the disobedience of the one man the many were made sinners, so also through the obedience of the one man the many will be made righteous" (Romans 5:19). Paul then goes straight into the reminder that we will slowly begin to see more clearly, that with God, "where sin increased, grace increased all the more" (Romans 5:20).

As you get to a place of acknowledging this storm and the secret, sinful desires of your heart, you will discover the sweetness in our suffering as we learn again, with deeper meaning, what it means to be "dead to sin but alive to God in Jesus Christ" (Romans 6:11).

Make this a prayer on your heart for the upcoming week. With the unraveling of all that is ahead, allow a small voice of hope to linger that reclaims over and over - dead to sin, alive in Christ. Believe in this hope; believe you will find peace as you see what it means in the second part of chapter 6 to become a "slave to righteousness" (Romans 6:18). Sin was defeated through the one righteous act of Jesus Christ, and you will find life again through defeating your sin as you become alive in God and remove the chains of sin.

When you question is there hope, scripture is full of it. No matter what people are saying about your marriage at this very moment. Their words and their thoughts aren't your identities. Their emotional responses may be filled with the condemnation that stings like truth, but it is not the truth. God will see you with a repentant heart even if the people around you only see a malicious one.

You will need God in this process more than you realize because there will be many times where He will feel like your only friend. He will guide you and direct the path ahead and keep you focused on maintaining an attitude like Christ in how you handle the middle of this storm and the choices you make through it.

Go to Romans, stay there as long as you need to, or make it your home until you get to a place where you can breathe again. Allow it to slow your heart, cling to God's assurance as we turn to faith in Christ on even the cloudiest of weather. With all the voices speaking into your life right now, God's voice needs to be the loudest and scripture will be the best avenue to hear him. Find encouragement in Romans 3:4 "Let God be true, and every human being a liar." Make decisions in line with the character of Christ and not just the voices of all your family and friends telling you the worldly responses of how to handle sin. Turn to your Father.

Here's an exercise to get you started on your hunt for hope.

/ / Exercise: Hope Hunt / /

Be on an active hunt for hope. There is hope in this seemingly hopeless storm, but much like an Easter hunt, you may have to look for it. It is right under your nose, so you don't have to go far, you just need to be more aware of your surroundings than ever before. This is an exercise to begin today with three parts to it:

Notecards

First, find a way to start jotting down and collecting the voices of truth in scripture, because the months ahead are going to be filled with voices of negativity that want to twist your mind from finding any healing.

I have been putting the scriptures that stand out to me on notecards, and I believe that one day they are going to serve as voices of truth to help even years from now. These verses are the word of God that should keep our hearts in line with the reminders of truth. My husband has even been caught sneaking my notecards when he finds a good one to add to the pile. I put a list of some of our favorite verses in the resource section to help you get started.

Journal

The second part of this exercise is to get a journal or a safe place where you can write some of the words you are hearing from other people. There are hard statements that people will say in the middle of the storm. Words that may have been or not have been said in love. They are painful to hear but said nonetheless. Words that you can't un-hear or unread in your life.

When you leave an encounter with someone, jot down the phrases that stick out to you that they said. These statements will serve as reminders of the sensitive place you are at right now. Words that months from now you may forget. Small and big voices may have a significant impact on your recovery story as it begins to unfold. There will be some voices that are negative and some that will be positive. As you move forward on your healing journey, you will gain better clarity on how to tell what is truth and what is not;

what is said in love and what is not. Discernment will increase as your character develops.

Identify Character Traits

The last section on our Hope Hunt will slowly connect you back with your spouse. The hope at this point is to get to a place where you have more good days than bad ones. And on the good days and the good moments, there are words and statements we will say to one another that we don't want to forget, even if we don't believe them right now. Whether or not you are getting a lot or very few positive statements from your spouse right now, write them down. You need them, and you will need to remember them in the months and years to come from your healing.

The three parts of this exercise I encourage both partners to be doing individually, people are talking to you both in this recovery time, or a sermon is sticking out, or a message on the radio, or a podcast, a phrase in a book, or even a song, through some avenue or outlet you both are getting advice and counsel. Hope is around you, you just might have to do some digging and some deeper noticing. Write out the statements that are sticking out in your mind, who said them, and where it came from. Your eyes, ears, and mind are open more than ever at this sensitive place in your life, let's take advantage of it!

Step II
SEE THE STORM

We've taken a breath, now let's see the mess, and stop the secrets.

Chapter 3
Recognize the Dust

Time to start with you. As we learn that we are both broken we also have to notice the vulnerabilities in our life that have impacted how we got to today. This is the path we need to start on, looking at ourselves before we are quick to point a finger. This is the time for us to understand grace, realize what forgiveness looks like even for ourselves, and turn from the path we have been on.

Dusty Sin

One of the household chores I hate the most is dusting. The one task that takes effort but goes completely unnoticed. No one has ever walked into my house and said: "Did you just dust? I can't believe how dust-free your furniture looks." My husband doesn't walk through the door and realize that the coffee table he's about to put his drink on just got wiped down. There is no pat on the back for dusting. People won't even know you did it. Almost as if our Christmas Elf on the Shelf stays with me all year long and helps with the mediocre chores that get completely unnoticed, wouldn't that be great? In reality, if the furniture is going to be dusted, I am going to have to do it. And why do I do it if nobody notices it has even been done? Because dusting is one of those chores that nobody realizes got done, but if you don't do it, that will completely get recognition. No one will say anything to your face, but people will notice the layer of dust on your furniture. We dust our houses because people see dirt, they don't praise cleanliness, but they see the dust if we don't take care of it.

Sin in our lives feels much the same way as dust in my home. If you don't keep up with it and continually work at keeping your heart pure, the dust will pile up to a thick layer that you can put a fingerprint in and will be noticeable to others. When we sin in a way that others can see, it will become all they see, and sometimes all we see in ourselves too.

We don't seem to get praise for living our life obediently in Christ, so if you are waiting for that recognition letter to come in the mail, you will be waiting a long time. There is no highlight when we are on the right track, but we get a spotlight when we get off course. Everyone notices the dust, and no one sees the hard work and all the times before this you have dusted and worked at keeping your heart clean. We recognize wrong more than we acknowledge right.

Recognizing your personal dust is in a sense admitting you are a sinner and in need of a Savior. The other recognition we have to make is that we are still sensitive to sins tug on our heart as the battle for our desires still wages on within us. Walking down a road you are not proud of can leave you still sensitive to that same road.

At this point in your marriage, you probably want a lot of answers from the storm you are currently facing in your home. You may have a million questions and want a bazillion answers, but the time for answers isn't now. Now is the time for recognition of where you both are and taking steps towards cleansing and healing.

> *Journal. I love you Lord my God with all my heart. I have fought to live my life with obedience and a cleansed soul, but I admit I have fallen short yet again. I want to be cleansed, I want to be restored, renewed, and refreshed. Help me to dust off the parts of my life that keep me from my first love, you.*

Recognizing the dust before we ask how it got there. Being a Christian doesn't make us immune to storms, it only makes us more equipped to survive them and boldly accept Christs' redemption plan.

When sin has a foothold in our life it makes us feel trapped, it makes us feel imprisoned by its grip and caged in a barred-up room.

It makes us feel those things, but truth paints a different story. Truth takes that cage and reminds you that the door is unlocked. You may feel stuck, but the way out is open. This truth comes from the fact that Christ came "while we were still sinners" (Romans 5:8). Christ didn't make himself lower than the angels just to figure out when He got here that we are all messed up, He came because He knew we were getting it wrong and He needed to be our solution. He came because the world needed to be dusted in a way only He could do.

We are all a work in process on a path towards sanctification. Realizing that you are a sinner, and really sitting in that truth is such a humbling position to put yourself in before your Father. When you reflect on your sin alongside a greater understanding of God's grace and love for your soul it is a beautiful and powerful position to sit in. The pain seems even deeper when you sit before the God you have committed your life to and go through the pain of admitting your current disobedience to Him. It is hard to let the people you love know you feel you have failed them, and even more so the God that loves you and the God in your life that you love as well.

Choices to be Made

When you fully give your life to Jesus and go through a storm of disobedience, things can feel hopeless and choice-less. You can feel like you've hit a dead end with nowhere to turn.

There are still choices you can make.

There are still next steps you can take.

There are still things to be done once you recognize the dust piled up in front of you.

You could be reading this for many different

Journal: I heard it said on the radio yesterday that "we can't fully understand the love of God until we sit in the understanding that we don't deserve it". Today God, I am learning the beauty of the Gospel, and recognizing the gift you've given me that I am learning in a new way, in an undeserved way, in a humble way.

reasons. You could be in the middle of your own awful journey. You could be hoping to gain a better understanding of a past sin or storm in your life. You could be reading it to help a friend that is struggling. Or, you could be reading it to be proactive for the fight ahead. Whatever your reason for turning these pages, I hope you find comfort and love in the middle of the dark storms, and begin to see the light as we dust the furniture residing in our hearts.

When we touch something dirty or messy, we are quick to wash our hands. After the mess of sin storms, there are choices to be made that will impact what next will look like. In the middle of your crisis, you need to hear that we can't go backward, and we can't undo, but we do have choices of what to do next. There are actually a few choices. As you read these suggestions, think through the choice you are leaning to and the choice you wish to have the strength to make:

(1) First, KEEP DOING IT. This is to continue in the sin. "Things around the house are already dusty, so why do something about it now?" Some people continue in sin believing it is wrong but telling themselves reasons why it might be ok. Others continue in sin because dealing with the weight of fault and turning away is hard. Repent and turn to God is no joke the hardest part in healing from sin-stains. I have watched way too many people lose the best parts of their life because they don't want to deal with the shame that naturally surfaces after admitting fault. Without believing that freedom can come out of shame, it is hard to get out of a lifestyle of sin.

(2) Second, DENY IT. This is to deny that anything ever happened or that anything is wrong. "I don't see a mess at all." People who live their lives compartmentalizing that a sin never took place, or finding reasons to justify it, so they don't have to deal with the repentance and restoration process that follows. They live their lives in denial, believing they have nothing they need to be redeemed from. They

create a reality in their mind where things are as they see them, which differs from the consistent sight seen by those around them.

(3) Third, OWN IT. I have seen people go two directions with owning it as well,

(3a) You can repent, find forgiveness, and feel freedom in being transformed, OR

(3b) You can repent, but struggle to find freedom from the label that gets connected with your sin. Adulterer, Addict, Pervert, just to name a few. Walking around with those new identities doesn't sound like freedom to me. Making a decision to own it without freedom from it is owning it to the extent that you don't know how to live your life without this label of sin attached to your skin. This path of owning it is admitting your wrongdoing, working through repentance, but feeling bondage by this sin as your new identity. It's owning the sin without freedom after repentance. Their identity becomes rooted in being a sinner instead of rooted in being redeemed. It's owning it without getting rid of the shame, and I'm just not convinced that Jesus died for our sins so that we could repent and carry them around with us the rest of our lives.

We all will reach a point where we hit this fork in the road, where we have a decision to make about sin in our life. Even people that struggle with jealousy, slander, greed, and gluttons, they all have to make a choice about what to do about the dusty sin in their lives. The storms of each sin may be different, but the choices are very much the same.

As you read the choices listed above, which one resonated the most with you? Here's an example of a couple that faced this same roadblock...

I remember working with a couple in my counseling office that went through a difficult season of anger with one another. Everything under the sun became a blow-out fight to a couple that once had communication as one of their top strengths. They began using their verbal strengths to hurt one another, and boy were they good at it. Since our sessions with them both in the room together weren't going anywhere productive, we did a few individual sessions so I could hear what was really going on.

At the surface for this couple was merely anger, but underneath all the yelling was decisions that each of them had made that they were ashamed of. Their personal shame was fueling the anger towards their spouse. They were each holding onto regrets of unfaithfulness and ugliness that they didn't know what to do with or how to break free from. Without even realizing it, they were masking their personal sin by finding things to hate about their partner so they could begin to justify their wrongful decisions.

This couple came to me wanting help with their marriage. But once I spoke to each of them privately, we were able to see they both needed personal assistance with their life first. There were choices in their daily lives that needed to be changed if they were to see any changes happen in their marriage. They needed to stop masking their sin and own it and find freedom from it. They needed to recognize their own dust and do some cleaning before we worked at cleaning the marriage.

Find the Opportunity

Sitting in this storm doesn't mean staying in it, it means getting to a place where we accept what's happened whether we like it or not. We need to know where we are starting to be ready to go anywhere else but here. Acknowledging our dust is being able to recognize that it is sitting right here in front of us and within us and something needs to be done. We will walk through the path and process of acceptance in the chapters to come, right now we just need to see ourselves in the middle of a storm, trust the process, and understand the truth and hope of storm stories of those that have gone before us.

I know that you are more concerned about what to do with the marriage right now. The marriage is crumbling, the marriage feels desolate, the marriage is getting the most criticism. I'm slowing you down in the middle of this crisis. Something needs to be done about the sin right now, then we can look at the marriage. I know you want to make a decision about your marriage, but first, you each need to look at yourselves, recognize the dust, and make a choice about what to do with the sin. Make a choice right now to: keep doing it, deny it, or own it.

With the struggle of restoring ourselves and repairing our marriage, we need to take full advantage of the opportunity this journey will give us. Yes, I said opportunity! You should be gaining small spurts of hope as you are learning you have a choice, and now you are starting to hear that this can be an opportunity of overcoming in your life. An opportunity to use this season to develop a stronger sense and understanding of the character of Christ. The battles we endure in our marriage don't need to be future war stories, they can turn into victory stories of overcoming in our lives.

To be profitable, our struggle must have a purpose, and it must be productive. "Two people who do nothing but fight in their marriage and make each other miserable are not engaging in a helpful spiritual exercise. It's only when we put struggle within the Christian context of character development and self-sacrifice that it becomes profitable" (Thomas, 2000). Finding opportunity means seeking a purpose through this storm. Need help getting started: start with using this as an opportunity to grow closer to Christ and envelop aspects of His character in a renewed way in your life. Another way to say that is to use this experience to walk out transformed from when you walked in. Make the beginning steps in this marriage crisis an effort of becoming more committed to a relationship with God instead of consumed with the things you dislike about your relationship with your spouse.

We need this grueling pain to mean something, for it to have a purpose, and for it to be productive for ourselves, our spouses, our families, and our marriages. I urge you, to journey through this storm and choose the path of making this struggle profitable and finding the opportunity in it. The struggle is real but believe with me that God has a plan for dusting the sin in the lives of individuals, relationships, and even groups of people throughout the actual stories in the Bible. God can grow us and our marriages through sitting in and going through what is up ahead, just don't forget that there is an up ahead.

Take a look around the house, and more importantly your life, do you see the dust? Make a choice on what you are going to do about it? (a) Keep Doing It, (b) Deny It, or (c) Own It. Let's keep going...

Chapter 4
Wildfire Secrets

In the middle of the storm, your marriage is in the traumatic puberty stage where it is has seen that something has happened, while slowly recognizing that something is happening, and that right now what's happening might not look too pretty. You look around and see a wildfire. A fire that is tearing down everything in its path. Later, we'll talk about the cleansing that brings new birth after a wildfire, but right now, your mind is cycling through the fact that you are in one. My guess is that somewhere in this storm, it started with a secret.

Journal: I miss myself from the past, just last year, I remember her smile, I remember a piece of her joy and I am wishing and hoping that in processing this out I might find it again, renewed and refined. Restoration can only take place through the strength that Jesus brings, I have heard this and preached it to others, but now is when God is looking me square in the eyes and preaching His Gospel message to me.

The Story Behind the Story

Every sin has a background story. There are details in our desires that entice us towards sin, and when our weaknesses line up with the wrong opportunity, we find ourselves in an environment set-up to a be the perfect storm. But no matter the perfect storm, no matter the excuse, no matter the circumstance, we always have a choice. Every sin has a story behind the story because the enemy is smart enough to wait and watch your world crumble to pieces.

There was a choice. Your marriage is where it's at today because someone made the wrong one, maybe even both of you did, and without hearing all the reasons behind the choices one or both of you have made, here is what I do know, I know there's more going on in your story than just what it seems.

There is a proceeding hidden story to the visible storms of your life, and wherever you are at, I want to start by modeling a place of compassion. Compassion that I don't have all the details, and in a position of trauma, you might not either.

Storms are filled with unknowns and are bred from the smallest of secrets. Some secrets will surface on their own, and some may stay hidden by master manipulators for years. Secrets are the missing pieces to the stories we hear in a counseling room, and the stories of confusion happening at your home. The danger in secrets is that this will become the breeding ground for the perfect storm. Secrets are the story behind the story.

There is a perfect storm part of the story behind most sin. Opportunity and vulnerability put us in a place that in our right mind we never fathomed we would be. We are all just one bad decision away from making the decisions we never thought we would make. It is these moments when you feel weak that the enemy will whisper destruction in your ear.

In my life, there are stories behind the stories I would have loved a weather forecast informing me that a storm was on its way. I would have secured all my belongings and gotten into a safe room in my house until the storm passed, but that's not real life. The reality is that we have God's word that describes in detail that every day we wake up and need to put on the armor of God (Ephesians 6:10-18) because there is always a storm brewing. Even on the sunniest of days, there is a war being waged for our heart. We are to always carry God's word as an umbrella when we leave our house, not just on days when we think it might rain, every day. Every day can present itself with a perfect storm situation, that could lead to its own set of regrettable decisions.

Wildfire Secrets

Just as some of the most deadly, unexpected storms, can occur from the rapid pace of a wildfire that is ignited from the smallest match, we also see some of the most significant sin storms that happen in our homes that have started from the most minor of secrets.

"Can you keep a secret?" I remember being asked that as a kid. You only told your deepest secrets to the people in your life you fully trusted. Secrets were either kept secret by the people you learned you could trust, or they were exposed, and you realized you would never tell that friend anything ever again.

As a teenager, telling a secret was a huge deal. It slowly gave you an avenue to show people a piece of yourself, a crush, or a confession. Rarely do we share secrets we are proud of, we tell people secrets that we either aren't ready to make public yet or things we wrestle with in our mind and just want someone safe to talk to.

As a child, secrets were a way to practice vulnerability. We whispered the bits about ourselves that we were still processing into the ear of our closest friend. "I like Johnny"; "I wish my family had money"; "I hate my step-dad". Whispers of the thoughts that have been swirling around in our head said out loud as a secret as a way of seeing if it was really true. They may start off harmless, but secrets can breed disaster.

We almost whisper half-truths just to try them on. It can be a crush in grade school but can morph into secrets about where to get the next 'drug hit' when you get older.

Secrets tend to need more secrets, which is what we are calling a wildfire of secrets. There is danger in secrets because anything done in secret is usually the thing in your life that will ignite a wildfire of secrets that become hard to put out. Many storms are difficult to go through, but if you've ever experienced a wildfire, you've seen the devastation that quickly destroys everything it touches. This is the environmental reality of a relationship that is filled with secrets.

For whatever the reason, secrets are not always as innocent as they mask themselves to seem. It is in the dark and quiet places in our lives that secrets tend to slowly spark a flame in our soul. It is in the secrets that we don't want anyone to see that we begin to lose control over our lives.

Secrets Breed Destruction

Secrets can seem innocent or juvenile when they start, but wildfire secrets will rob you of joy because wildfires are where our enemy, whose aim is destruction and isolation, likes to whisper back. The enemy aims to make the fire more prominent and to cause chaos on everything this firestorm touches.

His voice may sound caring, but we quickly forget that there is a war that has been waged among the desires of our heart. When you believe the lies that have been whispered in secret, it will create bondage on your life, and bondage is no way to live. Bondage tells the lie that you are helpless to win a war that's already been won.

Secrets and lies may be the cast of the most popular television shows, but they create wreckage in our homes, and they don't produce the life that brings us our happily ever after. But here you are, your life and your marriage feeling in bondage, and feeling like a television studio has set-up cameras in your home as they film their next big hit.

"How did we get here?" is the question flooding your mind right now. Bondage starts with a spark, and excuses for your secrets can be one of the biggest sparks you didn't see the harm in before this moment. Unrealistic justification will surface in the shadows of all your secrets. And when you start to find excuses that justify a toxic behavior in your life, this is when others notice that you are believing the enemies lies that have been whispered to you in secret. This is when excuses, alternate realities, and a world existing off of lies will all take shape when secrets take over your life. When we believe sin is justified, here's a few examples of what that might look like in your life:

-It doesn't matter what I do, it's not like anyone cares.

-I'm not hurting anyone else.

-I deserve this in my life.

-It will only happen this once.

-No one will ever know.

-If this is my biggest problem, they should consider themselves
lucky.

These lies are the sparks that give fuel to your secrets. They are diversions that keep us off track, and far from the morals we usually hold firm to. They are secret sparks that may start off as a whisper, but false whispers can influence the decisions you make next. In your marriage, believing a lie will spark a wildfire sin storm where "one night" turns into two, and where "one drink" turns into five, and where "one text" turns into an emotional and physical connection.

I have witnessed how the world of secret storms consists of a poison that distorts the very reality of some of the strongest, kindest, and friendliest of people. A twisted poison that will turn us into someone no one will recognize. Poisonous actions like revenge affairs are happening because spouses are feeling entitled to create their own secrets once their partners' sin has been brought to the light. A revenge affair is when one partner feels the only way they can understand and get back at their spouse is to treat them the way they were treated. "I should cheat because my spouse did it." Do you see how scary the whispered voices of secrets and unrealistic justification can be in your life? They are haunting voices, and they will feed each of you lies about how you should conduct your life.

Secrets breed destruction. And your marriage right now feels like destruction. It feels like a wildfire that might still be spreading. You are here because of some sort of secret. Some kind of secret that ignited a fire that needs to be put out. For you, that can be an exposed secret that already came out, a secret you know you need to share, or some of you are hearing whispers right now for the next secret to begin in your life. This chapter is about recognizing there is a fire in front of you, and before we start itemizing how to put it out, I have to make the plea for you both to not let it spread! "No evil dooms us hopeless except the evil we love, and desire to continue in, and make no effort to escape from" (Eliot, 2002). You need to escape from the flames not fuel them any higher.

Your secret may be the business trip that turned into an encounter with another person you are ashamed to tell your spouse about. Your secret can be an addiction you've told people you've stopped, but keep hidden in the shadows thinking you aren't hurting anyone. Your secret could be a lie that has been going on for so long that it's hard to say the truth. It could be that abortion done in secret years ago that is still waking you up in the middle of the night. Your secret could be the unresolved abuse or neglect that someone close inflicted on you. Or, your secret could be the lingering desire to see what your other options are and sign up on a dating website while you are still married to your partner.

Secrets have happened, and without a desire to get out of the storms all around, secrets are still at risk to run the story behind the story. Secrets are the breeding ground for wildfires to spread.

These secrets may be weighing heavy on you and preventing you from living the life of joy you hear holy people talk about. But that's not you. You can't look at yourself or your marriage as righteous right now because in the middle of this storm all you see is the dirt.

Secret storms have imprisoned you long enough. It's time to see the sun beyond the clouds instead of being trapped by yesterday's mistakes and yesterday's choices. Tomorrow will bring a new today. It's time to put out the wildfire before it continues to spread. Make decisions today that prevent the fire from spreading. Start now. Start today. While we heal from the fire that happened, do everything in your power right now to prevent another spark from getting ignited.

Step III
RESPOND TO THE STORM

"Now what do I do?"
We've treaded lightly up to this point and now is the
time to respond. Now is the time to make some major
observations and find hope in the desolate places.

Chapter 5
Road to Recovery

"We have a strange illusion that mere time cancels sin. But mere time does nothing either to the fact or to the guilt of a sin. The guilt is washed out not by time but by repentance and the blood of Christ." The Problem of Pain, C.S. Lewis (p. 54,55)

After a storm hits help is on the way. Well, that is true in the case of a catastrophic storm in our world, but not so much our personal lives. In our society, the salvation army, red cross, medical professionals, volunteers, businesses providing donations, and even soldiers come in to help get things back on track after a devastating storm hits. Everyone seems to play a part in surrounding the victims of a storm with the care they desperately need at an unexpected time in their life. There is beauty in the aftermath of a storm in watching people band together. The saying, it takes a village, is never truer than watching an outside community come in and care for the needs of others. With all-hands-on-deck after a real environmental storm, a network of people are seen swarming in to love on strangers – this is how we respond to loving the hurting in our response to a storm.

While we love on the helpless and the victimized, we aren't really sure what to do with sinners. When a family goes through a medical emergency or the celebration of a new baby we are quick to put together a meal train, but when a couple undergoes the trials of infidelity, pornography, or addiction in their life we non-verbally say "good luck and call me if you make it through this so we can all hang out again". Even when the intent is present, to love on people and care for them through whatever storm they are in, it's hard to know what to say, and we don't know what to do, so you stay busy, give them space and pray for the best. We isolate couples that are hurting because we don't know how to care for them.

This may be the norm right now in the aftermath of a storm that takes place in our homes, but my heart wants to see this cultural shift changed in our world today. I see a future where we are empowered to love through the storms because we have so much hope of what can happen at the end. I see a future where we surround each other as equals respecting that all couples have storms they just look different. I see a future where we turn towards each other to model grace, hope, and love to the hurting marriages that feel isolated and backed into a corner. This is the hopeful future ahead.

How we get there, is first making an attempt at getting started. In your home, the path we must take as initial steps on the road to recovery is to (1) seek out counsel; (2) find safety while unraveling the details; and (3) understand sin and suffering while you begin to believe there is healing on the horizon. There is so much power in these three HUGE steps to take individually that will have even bigger repercussions on your marriage.

Today, you might be on the receiving end with support all around you, or you could be the couple going through a storm, and no one showed up. Your marriage has suffered this storm, and you both feel emotionally bruised and broken, and no one showed up. No friends from the church praying over your home, no red cross volunteers at the door, no soldiers guarding your heart against the next attack, and not even a business giving you a financial donation for the debt this sin storm is costing your family. Whether or not people showed up to love you through the pain you have both been suffering, it's time to get on the road to recovery, and if no one showed up at the door that knew what to do you may have to do some seeking for support instead of waiting on a meal train to get started.

If the helping community knows that one of the first steps to recovery after a storm is sending in reinforcements for support, then that's where we are going to start too.

Seeking Counsel

We need to talk about it, even though it's hard to talk about. We need to be able to turn towards each other in our marriage. That is the goal, but you need a safe place to process things out first. It's time to seek counsel. Wise counsel is my strong recommendation, and I want to encourage everyone impacted by this storm to receive it.

Do you remember being in school and your parents were worried about who your friends were? It was because they knew what you had to learn, that the people and friends you hang around are going to have a massive influence on the decisions you make and the person you become. As adults, and going through any major struggle, today becomes an extreme version of the same scenario. As you go through this process of healing and restoration, the people you surround yourself around will be important in the counsel you get.

When it comes to your marriage, surrounding yourself with people that want to fight for your marital future is what you need. Being around family and friends that encourage you to run to the back door as soon as possible doesn't give you the help you need right now. Your family and friends want what is best for you, but you alone will be the one left at the end of the day with the decision you make to fight, flight, or freeze in your marriage. If you make that decision prematurely, it will be out of the emotions you feel right now at this sensitive place in trauma. Without further healing, any major relational decision made at this point will only be reactionary, not revolutionary.

There was a woman who gave me a great example of gaining worldly counsel. While having a year-long-affair that her husband was unaware of, she secretly began going to counseling to talk to a professional about the relationship she was in. Looking back, she is able to consciously identify that as a Christian she deliberately found a secular therapist, feeling quite aware that a Christian counselor would give her the advice she didn't want to hear which is to get out of the affair. She ended up being right, the secular counselor gave her the words she wanted which was to stay in both relationships while she figured out which man was the better choice for her life. These are the voices and advice of the world, they are not in line with the character of Christ, and we need to question whether the words of help we get from the world matches what the word of God says in this fragile point of recovery.

Professional Christian Counseling is my strongest and biased recommendation as it will help you gain a third-party perspective aligned with the words of Christ and the promises of God for your hope-filled life after this storm. I am sure that most of your friends are probably amazing, and they will be there to support and love you to the best of their ability, but that doesn't mean their positive intent is going to match their personal advice. Pretty much, I want you to hear that you are sensitive to advice right now in the middle of your marital crisis, so be cautious where you receive it. Talking to a professional who has the experience of helping others, and knows the long-term outcomes of the decisions you are both about to make is going to give you the best counsel right now. Family and friends are great at giving you comfort and making you feel better in the moment because they don't want to see you hurting, but they aren't usually the best to provide you with clear insight as to what decision you make today will be the best for your marriage long-term.

A professional setting gives you the safety of being able to openly talk about what has happened with a person that is emotionally unaffected to the hurt that has been caused. They may be the only person at this point that can see the whole picture beyond just the here and now that you, your family, and your friends are stuck in. Finding a Christian setting to do this in will provide you with the words that may be hard for you to hear, but will give you counsel that lines up with the character of Christ. I know that your instinct might want your reactions and responses to go against your morals, but a Christian professional can help redirect you to stay in line with your morals so that the journey out of the storm isn't filled with more regrets and side storms along the way.

When you bring the wrong people in to give you advice it has the potential to sway you away from making a rational decision. Our friends want to support us by telling us things that confirm the feelings we already have. They see you hurting and want to protect you more than they want to protect your marriage.

Also, talking and confessing about the sin brought into your marriage to anybody who will hear it is never uplifting for your relationship, not at this emotional stage. You will put your marriage in a position that makes it harder to heal and recover because you have only displayed the worst of this person to the world. Think of a safety net of people that will be good to know everything going on without telling everyone you know what is going on.

Your spouse may have hurt you by not protecting your marriage, and I will reiterate this over and over, that now you have a choice. Choosing to tell everyone of your spouse's sin in a vindictive verses productive form while you both are still at this emotional state is now you at a point where you are not protecting your marriage either. I cannot stress enough how gaining the correct counsel is imperative in helping to get the assistance you both need in the recovery journey you are going down. Remembering that sin has a story means also noting that your reaction to sin will have a story as well.

Find Safety While Unraveling the Details

The other benefit in professional counseling is that to fully get through our major sins we need a safe place to talk about the details. As I told you to be cautious of the family and friends you speak to, there needs to be someone in your life that knows the whole truth. Keeping in the fact that there are still secrets, and that you haven't entirely said everything out loud will consume and eat at you, and that's not our goal in this process of healing, and that's not what God wants for your life either. Full vulnerability in a safe setting can be healing, but screaming all the details to people as if it is your identity will make it hard to find freedom once this storm passes.

God will be with you through the whole storm, and as you uncover the entire truth. Redemption isn't offered for only half the story, all of it is covered. Gain healing from all of it as well. You are more than your worst day and more than your biggest regret, you are more, because you are His. His plan is not that you endure this storm, but that you find life through the storm. Having a safe avenue to discuss all the details is essential in your personal recovery. The emphasis here is on safety. Both of you should have that gift, to be able to share in safe settings without slander and external voices being brought into the mix on the ugly and regrettable parts of your life. There is already enough of an attack at work in your marriage, bringing in unsafe voices to the forefront will create distance and shame more than healing and recovery.

Disclosing to your Spouse

Deciding how much you share with your spouse is probably a struggle in your mind. Every circumstance and situation is different so determining the answer to this is hard to do in a general form, but what I do believe is that you need a safe place to go through your actions and the sin that welcomed this storm into your home so that you can thoroughly go through a process of healing. The person that has been hurt needs a safe place to talk through the pain and trauma they are experiencing as well. Without a safe place for that, you will both find yourself redirecting all your emotions towards each other in a way that may cause future harm that could result in sequential storms to arise in your marriage. This storm has been hard enough, let's commit to doing everything we can to calm the weather and not provoke it.

When it comes to deciding on what to disclose to your spouse, there are differing viewpoints on the necessity and severity of whether to reveal all the details to your spouse during the healing process. I have seen couples go through several forms of this and have seen each of them play out in different directions. I am not sure I have an exact opinion on this yet as I see personalities and circumstances have a different definition of what "disclosing the details" fully means. There are some that want a full confession, fully – nothing left out. When this is done while they are still at an emotional state, I have watched a confession meant for healing be used for leverage as the other person is making plans towards divorce. In this scenario, the more you share, the more ammo they have. This can be destructive.

My estimate of detail sharing has a lot to do with timing and safety. Without safety people don't seem to be listening to your heart, they only see your sin. And the timing has a lot to do with God's intervention. Two people on a path of healing may have two different timelines. Getting those timelines to sync up with God's active work on one heart and His active work in another will bring the fruit to allow some of the hardest conversations you thought you both would never be able to get through. When timing is divine, it can't be planned for, but it can be prepared for.

I would go so far as to argue that a forced confession, where safety is completely breached because you give a human being no choices, along with forcing your timing on them, is putting them in a traumatic situation. Forced confessions also send the signal of worthlessness. When we deem a person worthless, we take away their rights as a human being. Instead, done out of love, are signs of waiting for timing and giving safety, this is how we can actively love sinners. A full confession can be a huge part of healing, but being mindful of safety and timing will determine if the confession is being used as a detriment or a step towards recovery. It's great when you can at least tell your spouse that you'd "like to be able to tell them everything" as long as we can understand it more as an unraveling process than a stamped "date of confession" on the calendar.

The other hard part, as you will see in a later chapter, is that the person that has committed an exposed sin will have a hard time going through details if they haven't gone through their own path to acceptance yet. Acceptance and safety seem to be critical components in a person deciding whether or not they are ready to unravel the details. This explains why in a counseling room we don't get full disclosure on the things we are helping people work through until a couple months into counseling. The issue is often bigger than the depiction they presented in the first session.

Within themselves, they are working towards accepting the details to the point of being able to say it out loud along with scanning if the information they already gave the counselor was safe. A client will test out some of their story while observing how the counselor responds to what they've already disclosed. It is a version of the client examining, "Is it safe to tell you _____?"; "What about _____?". Are they shown love or condemnation? The answer to that question will play a large role in whether or not they share more details or give a full confession both in the realm of counseling and to their partner.

This is the pattern we see and prepare for in a counseling setting. We show consistency in support, care, and guidance, no matter the detail. Safety and security build trust, and the same happens at home as well. Unraveling the details to one another may happen a bit at a time as you both are in a state of not just showing that it is safe but also learning how to practice safety at the same time. Safety in being vulnerable is a new thing you are both getting used to, it doesn't happen right away, but it is worth the wait to show someone you care. Again, I am not saying if it's not safe don't tell your spouse, I just believe that timing plays a vital role in healing. A confession does need to be made so that repair can fully happen in your marriage, but the extent of details is a delicate matter that has the potential to both hurt and help.

Processing Through Confessions

Admitting a sin out loud can be more like peeling an onion, multiple layers and a lot of tears, this is why I keep referring to it as an unraveling process. One person can only say the parts of the sin that have been accepted, and then a new layer will come off, so more tears will unfold. Some people may be able to do it all at once, but my experience is that this becomes dependent on where your level of acceptance and ownership in your sin or the trauma that took place is at. Chances are if you were caught in sin instead of making a choice to disclose it on your own, you probably weren't ready to admit everything the moment you got caught.

Our sinful nature puts us in a place where we only admit to the extent that we got caught, and nothing more. Much like getting caught speeding on the highway, when the officer catches you going twelve over the limit, I'm sure the first thing you say to him isn't going to be, "Man I am glad you didn't get me on this same road yesterday when I was going twenty over the speed limit". The heart of the sinner is going through a lot, and there is no perfect picture of getting out of the tornado of sin we walk into. Confessions are a bit more of an unraveling process than an in-and-out hospital procedure.

You may be at a point where you both want to go straight into marriage counseling. This is actually the place where counselors would advise you both to begin with individual healing before being ready for marital counsel. Through the storms in my marriage, we gained the most benefit from seeking individual counseling at first, and it actually brought on some great conversations that we had together at home. We were learning, examining, and processing our emotions and reactions in a safe place that was non-destructive and it allowed us to come to each other with greater clarity and maturity in our interactions with each other. Our experience was doing two months of weekly individual sessions before our counselors believed we were ready for joint sessions together. Personally, I even benefited from EMDR specialized trauma therapy to help me deal with some sensitivities I have that are related to traumatic experiences I went through in childhood, adolescents, and into adulthood that manifested during the trauma of our marital storms. Working through my past unresolved pain helped me talk about the current issues I was working through.

With clients I have worked with, I have observed the same to be true. They are in crisis. They are in the middle of a storm that is suffocating their existence. They come into a counseling room together, and instead of finding healing, the fifty-minute session just sounds like a tornado of hurtful words and blaming voices attacking one another. The sensitivity in the room is so flared that nothing productive gets accomplished. In crisis mode, nothing exists except the here and now. All we end up spending the counseling hour talking about is who is bleeding the most instead of picking up the first aid kit and treating the wounds. Starting off individually allows for healing to be done and breaths to be taken before we all sit in a room together.

Sin and Suffering

To gain the life God wants for you to live, we have to go through the pain, and pain cannot be avoided. "We can ignore even pleasure. But pain insists upon being attended to. God whispers to us in our pleasures, speaks in our conscience, but shouts in our pains: it is his megaphone to rouse a deaf world" (Lewis, 1940). Sin will always lead to some form of pain, this is why God instructs us away from it to begin with. I know you were taught to never use the words 'always' and 'never', but I am using it, sin will always never fail in leading to pain and suffering. Good cannot come from destruction on its own, but God can turn our destruction into good, that is just one of the blessings of overcoming the world!

God didn't give us rules because he wants to torment us with obedience, but because he is trying to save us from suffering. Now that God has our attention let him use our pain as a magnifying glass for what he wants to show us through it.

God as Counselor

If I were to talk to my television screen during a scary part of a movie, I would shout to the characters, "don't go down that dark alleyway...duh...good things will never happen". But they won't listen to me, they're going to walk down that alley, and I can either cover my eyes or see the suffering they are about to go through. The movie usually has a rescue plan, but not always. So how does God deal with us walking down that dark alleyway that the Holy Spirit yelled in our ears "Don't do it"? He uses it in the formation of our character. He never wanted you to walk down that alleyway into sin, but you did it anyway. He also doesn't leave your body there to rot. It won't be fun to get out, but God will use this to develop and shape you. Romans teaches us: "suffering produces perseverance; perseverance, character; and character, hope. And hope does not put us to shame, because God's love has been poured out into our hearts through the Holy Spirit, who has been given to us" (Rom. 5:3,4).

Just like some of the most uncontrollable circumstances in life, like a child dying, or a loved one getting a physical disease, or hearing that someone close to you was killed by a drunk driver. All of those horrible situations are painfully difficult for anyone to go through, but the people that have had to go through them either lose themselves or develop a tremendous amount of character they would not have known without this pain and suffering. This process of suffering through sin in your marriage God can use too, but we have to go through it the right way. The suffering from sin you are both sitting in is difficult to bear. Remember that the night can only get so dark, and then there is dawn. There will be a day beyond this one, and a day after that one as well. That is constant, that's not going to change. What's going to change now is you, and your marriage. It will never be the same, and you won't either.

The character you will develop will depend on the path you travel ahead.

Whether you both make decisions that will put you in a position of being closer in your character to Christ or in line with your already sinful nature, that is the decision and level of obedience you get to choose. Choosing to imitate Christ in dealing with the existence of sin will have the most beautiful outcome in you as a person.

You and your spouse may be on different pages right now, and the future seems unknown and hard to even think about, but individually, what I know to be best for you both is to make the next decision act in line with God's plan of finding life after sin. Gary Thomas talks about the examples of people that had suffered much in their marriage and personal life, but through it all these sufferings shaped their character and made them the influential people they were or gave them the marriage they wouldn't have had otherwise. He goes on to talk about the benefits of going through suffering that is hard to notice at the time. He stopped me right in my tracks when he asked the readers to "ask yourself this question: 'Would I rather live a life of comfort and remain immature in Christ, or am I willing to be seasoned with suffering if by doing so I am conformed to the image of Christ" (Thomas, 2000, p. 108)

What a question to consider. The decisions next to be made in the suffering that lies before you both could be looked at from such a different viewpoint if we believed that God can do something through suffering. Thomas explains this perspective shift by saying that "it helps when we view our struggles in light of what they provide for us spiritually rather than in light of what they take from us emotionally" (Thomas, 2000, p. 128). The power in that statement almost stings as we want nothing more than to let our emotions take over our reactions and responses to everything around us. Both spouses need to filter everything they think and feel right now. You need to see past the lens of not just how every decision effects the marriage you are not even sure you want right now but looking at only you and God, each of you.

Ask yourself this in the coming weeks: How is each decision and every encounter you have with one another going to benefit me spiritually? Beginning now, with the difficult steps ahead, ask God with the most scared and vulnerable heart you have at this moment, to care for you, and that through the pain and whatever happens to the future of you and your marriage, that you and God grow closer to each other through the storm.

// Exercise: Road Blocks //

Take a look at your life right now and look at the obstacles popping up that you feel are in the way of you taking the three critical steps we talked about in this chapter: (1) seeking out counsel; (2) finding safety while unraveling the details; and (3) understanding sin and suffering. I know there is a wall of excuses and even a wall of real-life circumstances ("I have to work," "I don't have time for this," "I'm not the one with the problem") that makes taking action on a few of these steps hard to actually do. Remember that we are on the Road to Recovery, but what is the point in being on a Road if you don't take any steps to go down it? There is promise up ahead, but to get up ahead, you have to lift up your feet one after the other. For every obstacle weighing down your ankles, there is an answer, you just need to pray about it and find ways to overcome it. Do the exercise on the following page to help you think through the three major steps on your Road to Recovery right now, list out the things that you feel block you from taking this step, and also something you can do to break down that barrier. I've put together a table chart to help you with this exercise on the next page.

Exercise: Road Blocks

	ROAD BLOCK	BREAK THROUGH TACTIC
(1) Seek out counsel (Gain wise advice)		
(2) Work on Unraveling the details (with safety)		
(3) Understand sin and suffering believing there is healing on the horizon.		

Exercise: Road Blocks *Example*

	ROAD BLOCK	BREAK THROUGH TACTIC
(1) Seek out counsel (Gain wise advice)	*Financial – I just don't know how I am going to afford a Counselor right now.*	*I will start by exploring the options in my area and see if I can find a resource that can help me, or offer a sliding scale for services.*
(2) Work on Unraveling the details (with safety)	*I don't even know where to start, I don't feel safe talking to anybody right now.*	*I can start by journaling what I am able to say right now, I can start with writing things that I am having trouble saying about my life.*
(3) Understand sin and suffering believing there is healing on the horizon.	*I can't even begin to believe in healing right now! I am so consumed with hatred and anger.*	*I can begin to see what God sees when He looks at a world filled with disobedience and sin. I can look in God's word and hold onto the promises that are hard to believe right now in my life.*

Chapter 6
Assessments

As the first responders sweep in to help with the aftermath of a grand storm, at the top of their list is to make an assessment of what's been done, what needs to be done, and prioritizing the needs. Finding ways to organize in the middle of a disaster is a skill, a skill even I need to develop as I walk in to clean up the kids' playroom. With a mess that most people will deem too overwhelming to fix, a hopeful eye can step in, see potential, and see a way to organize the chaos. This is the blessing and training of first responders, they come in and see more than just a mess – they understand where to start.

Without assessing the needs, there are a bunch of willing hands all running around in different directions. Instead, the best recovery from a storm happens when many hands are headed in the same direction. Making an assessment of the damage after a storm is a critical first step. Without knowing the condition of our current surroundings, we may run the risk of still being in the wake of a storm with dark clouds on the horizon. Assessments give us clarity in chaos. They are necessary to move forward with repairs. They provide structure to disaster, and a plan to deal with unexpected intrusions.

If assessments are valuable in critical storms, it's time for us to make this personal and do an evaluation on the storm that just blew through, or is swirling around in our marriages today. As we look inward to our own struggles, let's also take a look outside ourselves at the damage that's been caused by looking at (1) what's been done; (2) what needs to be done; and (3) prioritizing the needs.

What's Been Done?

The phrase What's been done? is different than the instinctual response of Who did it? The expression Who did it? is where you might want to start. The problem is that when you start there, it's also where you are going to want to stay. Finding where to start has a lot to do with starting with the right question. When the first question begins with a "who" it tells us right away we need a heart check.

Many doctors don't even know the name of the patient they are about to work on, they focus on (1) what's been done, (2) what needs to be done, and (3) prioritizing the needs. If doctors spent lengths of time in the conference room before a major surgery blaming all the leading factors that caused a person to be laying there on their operating table, then, by the end of their meeting, that patient may not be breathing when they walk in to operate. When our marriages are in crisis, that same truth can be happening in your home. Spending too much time starting with blame and contributing factors can ignore the relationship that is on life support on the operating table before you.

I hope that metaphor is helping you see that the first question can't start with "who" in a crisis assessment, it needs to start with a "what". When the first question we ask starts with a "who" the next thing we are likely to say will begin with a "you". When we spend our time talking about "who did this" our energy will fixate on blame, and blame is not a solution, just a leading factor to how they got on the operating table. "Who did this?", can quickly turn into "You did this!", which will follow with a "what are YOU going to do to fix it?".

Did you follow all that? When we focus on "who" it will point us to a "you", and we will look for "you" to be the solution.

When a "you" becomes the solution to a storm, we point our finger at a person and not a storm. While the aftermaths of a storm have the potential to bring people together, the aftermath of sin can tear people apart without intentionally starting with the right question. While sin leads to destruction, we can work to see it like a storm, and in unity, work on the repair that brings order into the chaos.

If a storm were a person, they would get punished. We would respond to the perpetrator storm with a responsive attack. That's how a storm would be handled if it was a person. You hurt me, and now I am going to hurt you. But a storm is not a person. Sin is not a person. People give in to sin, people engage in sin, people can live a sinful lifestyle, but they as a person are not the embodiment of sin. We can't treat a person like they are a sin, but we can work on realizing that a storm is a faceless enemy even if you want so desperately to give it a face. That is a process more than a decision, but making that decision is a step in the process.

Don't get me wrong, sin needs to be dealt with in the full reality of what it was and renouncing its claim any further – but if we believe a sin is a person which also implies that a person is a problem, we are at the wrong starting point. "You did this, you fix this" may be normal in the way we live our everyday lives, but I am not convinced it's the way Jesus wants us to live in our marriages (we'll unravel that a little later). Separating a "who" from the "what" is our starting battle in this crisis assessment. As long as the problem is a "who" and not a "what", we are complaining around a conference table about leading causes when what we need to be doing is surgery.

Blame may be the initial response, but a crisis assessment will be a productive response. The first productive question needs to be what's been done?. Blame attacks the person, but What's been done? acknowledges that you are both a person, something just happened, and something needs to be done.

An example of blame in this immediate response is being too quick to respond with "I sinned because you _____". Another angle is responding with "You sinned because you are a _____". If you put an unpleasant label in there, know that you need a heart check as you get started. And if you filled in that blank with an unpleasant label about your spouse, that might help you see that you just may be a sinner as well. Whether your spouse is a "bad" person or not, saying they are bad because of _____ is a label that is hard to undo for the way you see them and the way they begin to see themselves in the days and years to come. Once someone starts making condemning responses, new damage will be done, and it will be damage that we may have to add to our personal assessment sheet when we are ready to be honest with ourselves.

In the aftermath of a storm, asking What's been done? is stepping outside for a moment to notice that a storm just blew through. For one, or both of you, it allows you to start seeing the effects, noticing the damage, and being sad that it is there.

After the existence of a physical storm in our community, asking what's been done is acknowledging the basics – earthquake, tornado, fire, lightning. It answers the question: What just happened? In our marital sin storms, this is where we add labels – storms of sexual immorality, physical and/or emotional abuse, unfaithfulness of some kind, addiction, rage/anger, slander, pride, and the list goes on. In this part of the assessment, we start with making acknowledgments and checking all the boxes of what just blew through. No blame, just checking boxes. Surely there was enough blame that already took place before you got to this chapter, so now let's focus on the what's been done so we can move forward with making observations on what needs to be done.

What Needs to be Done

When I have car trouble, I describe the problem as if I am playing a game of charades. I don't have the knowledge to mention the names of meaningful parts in a way that a mechanic or even a basic human being who listened in drivers-ed might use. Instead, I come up with my own language, even my own sounds and hand gestures to get my point across.

As we head into our next question, it can seem like we are about to play a game of charades. Asking What needs to be done? about sin, storms, emotions, and the present state of your marriage can all feel like descriptions for a vocabulary you don't have, or may not be comfortable using right now. You see the problem, but it's hard to describe it, hard to put into words exactly what needs to be done. You know the car isn't working, but you don't know how to tell the mechanic exactly what it is that needs to be fixed. No wonder your marriage feels hopeless in this season, your mind doesn't know how to describe what is happening, all you see is a car that won't start.

What needs to be done? encourages us to look at ourselves, and our marriage right now, and make observations based off of what we can see and the vocabulary we do have. In the wake of a traumatic story, forming sentences doesn't come easily. Clarity will come as the fog lifts, but at this moment, take note of what you see in the fog.

A community would answer this part of the assessment by making observations of power outages, trees blocking major roads, and so forth. In the aftermath of the storm you are surviving let's start asking the same questions. An example of What needs to be done? may be that trust is gone. Trust may be the current power outrage that is out of service in your home right now. Hope seems fleeting. Dreams are shattered. Hearts have been broken. A self-image has been distorted. These are all examples, your words may be different. Your words may be consistent in describing that the car isn't working. You may say things like "something doesn't feel right between the two of us, something I don't think can be fixed". In your list of observations, you may be saying things like, "I don't feel like we are connected anymore," and "I've lost hope." That may be all your vocabulary can muster up. At this part of the crisis assessment, just make observations of what you see and how you feel.

As you answer this part, getting it right and labeling it correctly isn't the objective, right now just make observations based on what you see and the words you are able to form together. It will shift and change as you move forward in healing. Your life is in a place of crisis right now, so forming perfect words that neatly package how you feel and what's been lost in the rubble may feel impossible. Just think through what you can muster up at this point in the healing process, the both of you, and more words will come as you move forward.

Prioritizing the Needs

As your list of observations grows, your surroundings may feel more disorganized than ever. Here's the step in our assessment where we tackle the most pressing needs. We look at the storm like a patient coming in from trauma – we assess the situation and get treatment for the most severe conditions underway to maintain life as the body heals.

Now is when we take our list of acknowledgments and observations and prioritize the needs. Do we clean the roads or deal with the power outages? Making these decisions will keep us focused on the mess of a storm left behind, but picking up the pieces will be determined by needs of necessity or proximity. Necessity says we need it for survival – things like safety, hygiene, self-care. Proximity says our direction is led by whatever is in front of us. Prioritizing off of proximity can be driven by our emotions, and directed by whatever is the biggest problem at that moment. When we clean up with proximity, we may run out of oxygen to breathe because we are too busy putting a cast on our leg. Prioritizing proximity says it's important to walk, prioritizing necessity says it's more important to breathe.

In this last part of our assessment, when we Prioritize the needs, our focus is on survival, and then later we will prioritize a full revival. As you begin prioritizing the essentials for your marriages' current survival state right now, you want to think through prioritizing ways to minimize your risks for another storm. Here's a little help to get you started: prioritize seeking support for the both of you; prioritize having rules of respect in the way you communicate about all this, and think about ways you can prioritize your health right now. There are a lot of wounds that need to be attended to, remember that this part of the assessment is just prioritizing the top survival needs right now. Both of you may have different definitions of what is most important, my main concern is safety, and then try to see what you both come up with to prioritize the marriage to survive right now.

/ / Exercise: Marital Damage Assessment / /

Today, we will focus on today. Each of you take some time to fill in the blanks of your observations right now. If you have trouble starting here, do this exercise on a separate piece of paper to get you started. As you answer these three questions, answer them as best you are able to right now, even if you have to leave things blank or if you end up writing too much. After some time passes, do this exercise again and notice how your ability to make assessments will develop as your level of awareness and clarity increases.

1. What's Been Done?

HIS OBSERVATIONS	HER OBSERVATIONS

2. What Needs to be Done?

HIS OBSERVATIONS	HER OBSERVATIONS

3. Prioritize the Needs

HIS OBSERVATIONS	HER OBSERVATIONS

Chapter 7
Acceptance

We can't go much further talking about your marriage in crisis right now without gaining an understanding of the brain at work, and how our emotions and our mind are working overtime in the middle of this marital storm you are both in. There is a unique mind in each of us. We all may organize information uniquely, but what is the same, is that we are all organizing information. Without having to even think about it, the mind is at work thinking on its own. You may only see facial features and a nice pretty head, but under that layer of skin and beneath that thick skull, is a mind at work compartmentalizing all sorts of information.

Mental Anthills

Just like the sight of an anthill on the ground, all we see is a blob of dirt. We see the external features of a pile of dirt that give an illusion of nothingness, but under that pile is a process of organization, structure, and a system hard at work. The brain and the sight of an anthill have many similarities. Every ant has a job and a duty. Every ant has a place, and every ant is doing their part towards the same goal - protect the queen.

Your brain is very similar, and you are its queen. Every neuron is an ant at work bringing in information and doing what is necessary to maintain the health and environment for the queen.

We don't get to see the ants at work under the hill, we just know it is happening. But let's look at what happens when that anthill gets stepped on, or crushed – the breach of safety has just been signaled, and everyone has to stop what they are doing to move in to do damage control. All the moving parts are now focused on assessing the damage and assessing the safety of the queen. The system has been shaken. They scatter everywhere. Still with a job to do, but a job that falls under their damage repair job description.

This is a metaphor of your mind, and when sin has a foothold in your life, and a storm blows through, the brain will have a neurological response in that moment of crisis.

Traumatic Effects of Sin

Traumatic seasons in our life can be unexpected, and emotional trauma on the brain can flip your world upside down. Whether done intentionally or not, sin in our life can result in trauma to our brain. Even if we believe that people 'deserve consequences' to sin, we see the consequences and never know how to care for the person in the aftermath of trauma. There is almost a normality to watching people suffer the consequences of sin with panic and anxiety attacks, depression and signs of hopelessness, significant shifts in weight, eating and even changes in sleep cycles – these are the questions asked after a trauma when you visit the doctor's office. All of these behavioral symptoms after sin are noticeable, can be expected, and even medicated to alleviate their appearance. But more is at work than what can be seen, there are neurological responses after sin that also need to be cared for.

Whether you brought a sin into your marriage or were impacted by it, your brain is firing off synapses to process the information of trauma you may wish wasn't a part of your story right now. Faster than an ant can jump onto your leg and give you that irritating ant bite is the brain at work shooting off signals faster than you would know what to do with them. Your brain is overwhelmed and punching in overtime with all that is going on in your entire body.

Trauma and sin have a correlation, a correlation that is rarely discussed because we only talk about what we can see right in front of us. We see depression, and we are perplexed with anxiety, but the body and the mind are at work in the wake of trauma. In fact, trauma is one of the most tangible ways that we can see the real correlation between the mind and the body. They are a team, they influence one another, the mind and body rely on each other, and they will look to one another through this season of recovery.

The path to acceptance is difficult right now as the brain has work to do. Acceptance is a process, and there is a mental and physical process towards accepting the situation you both are in.

In my personal trauma education, we make observations as therapists in the way the mind heals from trauma. The model we conduct with trauma therapy is even different from a regular talk therapy session. In trauma recovery, we believe the brain is the master of its own work and has the ability and desire to heal itself. Even in a fallen world, we have a God that crafted us towards healing, how neat is that.

Trauma is a real thing, and as you take the path towards accepting your situation, there is a lot at work going on in your mind. You may think the brain is trying to make sense of everything because "What just happened?" is the question on repeat in your mind, but counter to that, is the reality that the brain actually doesn't need to understand everything to heal from it. You might want to recognize as much as you can, but understanding and recognizing are two different parts in recovery. What the brain needs is just space to explore the parts that are the most important to that person right here at this moment in time. The mind needs to look at the current, most distressing thought and needs the safety to process out an expression of hope about that experience. Doing it this way allows the brain to heal from one distressing part of the trauma at a time.

Responses after Sin

While the brain is at work protecting the queen, the body has emotional responses that you may have trouble describing. Even as I tell you that you don't need all the answers right now, I know your body has an instinct to want them. Our instincts want answers in the hopes that answers will free us from pain. This is not the case, but may entirely be what we feel. This book may even be your attempt at seeking answers to all your "why did this happen?" questions. On the hunt for answers, whether direct or discrete, your body and mind may show emotional symptoms as it responds and processes this current storm.

The path to accepting your present reality is your body and mind shifting into a new normal, a normal you never wanted, but a normal that becomes hopeful and expectant that something more is to come. Acceptance is a destination we have to get to, but on the path of accepting what we've done or what's been done, there are a couple other symptoms that creep in. You may notice yourself or your partner experiencing one, all, or none of the following symptoms. Just as hard as they are to go through, is realizing all the people that are hurt may be experiencing these symptoms too. Getting to the place of acceptance is a vital part not only for the person who has been disobedient in some way but to all your loved ones as well. It is only when we get to a place of acceptance (and forgiveness) that a fog begins to lift and we become more rational and realistic in how to move on from this in our life.

Here are some of the symptoms you may be experiencing or witnessing from those around you. The five that we are going to mention in this chapter are Shock and Denial, Anger, Bargaining, Depression, and Acceptance. As we go through each one together take note of what you are observing within yourself and what you are witnessing from others around you.

Journal: Acceptance is a difficult path to follow. My body wants to fight not wanting this to be a part of my story, the regret wants it to just go away, the hurt wants to live in another reality, but I know somewhere small inside me, that healing can be found through acceptance. I am learning to trust the process, and God will be faithful for the healing that follows.

Shock and Denial

Shock and denial can show their face in the aftermath or even duration of a storm. When we make agreements with sin, we can use denial as a mechanism of justifying our behavior. Denial helps minimize the effects of sin for what they really are. Denying wrongdoing is creating a world in our minds where we don't have to cope with what's been done or what's currently happening.

Shock and denial seem to immobilize us in place, so that forward doesn't even feel like an option. Standing still is about as good as you think your life is going to get. Options may not even seem feasible to you, and your life may even seem to be at an incredibly slow pace as nothing seems to make sense anymore. Denial says: "I don't believe it", and shock responds with "I can't believe it".

But why? Why do we respond with shock and denial? (Look at you, looking for answers again.) Remember that our mind will always try and protect the queen. We respond in ways that help us protect ourselves. Ourselves. Remember that. Our instincts create responses for us to protect ourselves, not our marriages. We have to make conscious decisions to protect our marriages, not always trust our instincts.

Confessions of Confessions

There are more reasons why shock and denial pop up as a protective measure. Along the path of shaking hands with sin, there are usually lies and agreements we made with sin that got us to the place we feel stuck at right now. (For these pages, we are defining agreements as the alignments and false beliefs we adopted that invited sin into our lives) There is even a distorted belief system or an escaped reality that seemed so real that coming back and waking up to the real world seems unfathomable. People are telling you to snap out of it, but repent and turn to God is not just an action you take, it is a strong-willed battle of the mind that is hard to let go of.

To move forward, you first have to acknowledge all the agreements you have made on your path to sin and aligning with new spirit-filled truth agreements on your way into freedom.

At the onset of confession, getting to the point of admitting sin out loud is a more difficult task than people realize. In the wake of the storms that others have walked through has been the realization after the fact that both individuals weren't entirely truthful at the initial confession. It was hard to be. It is hard to be honest with someone else about a truth you haven't fully acknowledged yet within yourself. There is a state of shock at even having to confess something you weren't proud of. At the initial confession, hopefully, you at least said out loud all you were able to muster up at that time. Having to give the admission of guilt in those initial stages of discovery is excruciatingly hard. Just as you are in shock at your spouse's confession, they tend to be in a state of shock in having to give one.

I know the last thing some spouses want to hear is how their anger and responses and reactions are affecting their partner. "I don't care if I hurt them, they didn't seem to care about hurting me" is the response I hear in a counseling room. Hurt people, hurt people. Sadly enough that statement has become so routine that we feel like it is inserted into a golden rule, but it's not. We aren't gifted with entitlement because of our spouse's sin, we can become cursed by it. These pages are meant to be your perspective shift in a culture that feels its ok to hurt people that have hurt you. We're pausing in the middle of our hurt, taking a breath, probably being angry, but trying not to clench our fists for a punch. When confessions take place or are requested, we can't shake our spouse until they tell. We need to view the stage of confessions as a process more than an interrogation.

As we walk further down the path to acceptance, a confession unravels slowly more than it gets dumped out all at once, remember the onion we talked about earlier. I know this is hard for the person who was hurt to hear, but the emotional reasoning behind it is that on the path to acceptance you are still wrapping your brain around the fact that you even did something to this extent. When you sit in the symptoms of shock and denial, the pace may seem slow moving, but seeing some movement is significant. Taking steps forward in accepting the ability to give a full confession and for your spouse to be at a place to hear it is the current goal.

What is hard for the impacted community of a torrential storm to hear is that recovery doesn't always happen on the timeline the city wants it to. Personal and marital healing after sin is just as similar, it is a process. If we know that sin is messy, why do we assume the path out would be any cleaner?

A storm that blows through our town can take a day to sweep through, but months, or even years, to repair. Healing and repair will be slower than you want, but worth it in the end.

In the sphere of counseling, we get used to slow vulnerability. We learn to expect it because we have witnessed the beauty of the long-term relationship of therapy. For people looking for a quick-fix in their life, it is easy to give up on therapy because people want short-term fixes for their long-term problems. But, how they resolve short-term fixes, is really their long-term problem. When we don't value the process in the long-term, we only make short-term impacts on our life.

Getting to see people unravel their pain, unravel their ownership, all happens under the context of safety. Remember the ant analogy, even in grief, even in trauma, we still seek safety, even when we are the one to blame. No matter the guilt we cannot dehumanize a person. When we dehumanize a person, we believe so firmly that we are right that we take away the rights of the other person. I can't do that to someone sitting across from me seeking help. I cannot! Instead, in therapy, we talk about what they are able to talk about, hoping they feel safe enough to talk about more at their own pace. When a counselor provides safety with someone, their mind can let go of the army forces guarding their walls, and it allows them to feel safe enough to explore a world beyond shock and denial. That is an example in the counseling room, the beauty of this comes when it happens in your home.

Counselors see vulnerability as a process, but if you aren't used to that mentality, you may view masked vulnerability as nothing more than a lie. "You lied to me." "That's not what you told me last week." In a state of shock and denial, it is hard to say the whole truth and honestly hard to hear it as well. This is precisely why in a mental state of feeling surrounded by the fog seeking answers isn't the answer, because you may not get the answers you are actually looking for, and you most likely dehumanized a beating heart on your quest for answers. Having to give confessions on a previous confession is hard as it can keep unraveling. We can change our ability to provide safety if we prepare for vulnerability to be a process more than a step.

The hope is that the state of shock and denial is a symptom that lasts only a season if you even have to go through it all. Never would you want to stay in a world that doesn't exist when real life is on the other side. Shock and denial may be an instinctual response, but recognizing its existence gets you closer out of the fog.

/ / Exercise: Name it / /

A great way to examine if you are in a place of shock or denial right now is to see what you are able to name and claim. This is a way of going further into your Marital Damage Assessment Form.

1. Are there any more parts of the storm you may be ready to own as you move out of shock and denial?
2. Are there any new observations of what needs to be done or even new prioritizations as you begin to see out of the fog?

As you name and say aloud new parts that were present in the sin storm more will be healed as more is let out into the light. Headed out of the shock and denial, be warned that more symptoms may surface at the same time.

Anger

There are other emotional reactions after trauma intercedes our

> *Journal: In my life right now, hatred lies where love once did, this seems to be the destruction of sin.*

life. Anger seems to be almost instinctual. When that car shoots in front of you in traffic...anger. Anger even shows up in the form of frustration as a child, when we don't even have the words yet to speak. In something as simple as the tone of someone's voice we can hear signs of anger. When my kids would scream as infants, I remember

Matt looking at me and saying, "It seems like he is screaming curse words at me". Anger.

Anger displays itself in many forms throughout our lives. Its expression and degree of passion are unique to all of us, but what we find to be central with anger is that it is a secondary emotion. When we feel anger, it is never the actual problem. Anger is a symptom of bigger issues going on in your life. As infants, our kids are trying to tell us something through their frustration of a bigger need in their life. They are hungry, in need of a new diaper, all statements they can't make, but anger breeds attention, and attention gives us hope for an answer.

Anger is really an expression of something bigger, but in the middle of anger, feeling angry makes us feel better, and then worse, and then better, and then worse. You get it. Anger is a natural emotion that we all experience, but one you need to be very careful because it doesn't usually have one directed target. When anger comes to the surface, it will be all over the place. Everything you are angry about will come out at different moments and different times in your life.

As you begin to acknowledge the presence of sin in your life on this path to acceptance, you may even find yourself starting with being angry at everything but yourself, and everything but your sin. This is where we have to make a conscious effort to turn our anger inward to the sin from our flesh, even when our instincts tell us to direct our anger outward onto someone else.

Turning anger inwards is becoming angry with the flesh, and often, trying to understand that your spouse is angry at you. The fog of shock and denial has lifted, and now, you get mad. You wish you could turn back the clock and do things differently. It's not a proud moment. This state of inward anger is not when you are looking for the good that God can make of this, you are just sitting with the ugliness of everything that has been done. You stare at the sin as if it were sitting in the chair next to you and begin to feel disgusted. Inward anger has to be looked at. It has to be addressed and dealt with, but how you deal with it will affect what happens next.

I am sure you have heard before, "it's ok to be angry, but what you do with your anger you are held responsible for", and here's a word of caution that goes along with that: For whatever next looks like for you and your marriage, you will be responsible and accountable for it. Anger is closely tied to future susceptibility to sin. There is no 3-month window after sin where your responses are entirely justified, you both are still susceptible to sin while you recover from sins ugly entrance into your home.

This means that how we handle our anger has the potential to set us up for an invitation for our own category 5 hurricane sin storm to makes its entrance, or can invite a gentle breeze in the wind. We have a choice in how to handle our anger. A choice! Again, instincts will point you in one direction, but you may find healing in the other.

What you do with your anger is something you need to be mindful of. The Apostle Paul gave an admonition that "in your anger do not sin" (Ephesians 4:26). My husband, Matt, and I have both been hurt by each other in our marriage, and we recall the anger associated with the hurt caused us both to have reactionary thoughts of wanting to hurt the other person or even flee. That's what it means for anger to creep in and take over us to the extent of making us susceptible to sin. Anger can quickly turn into contempt, and contempt will try to control our decisions. When anger has control, you will walk into a world that you may have to go through a new stage of shock and denial to get out of. You may become a person you aren't proud of. Instead of focusing our anger towards healing we can use it to fuel hurting the person that hurt us, this creates a whirlwind of more damage on our relationship.

With a soft, but stern heart, I want you to hear, that if you are not ok with your spouse justifying their behavior, please don't use their sin as a way to justify yours. Our human nature is that bullies tend to bully and people that have been hurt have a tendency to hurt. We have to push against that human tendency, and in a state of anger, you may not be ready to hear this yet, but coming ahead you will have to get unstuck from this stage to recognize that forgiven people also forgive people.

Stuck in Anger.

The state of anger is where I see the most individuals and couples get stuck on the course to healing. I have seen it over and over again where instead of anger being a season on the path to healing, it becomes your new lifestyle. Years of anger will distance you in your marriage and will lead to mutual hostility between you and your spouse. When a sin storm enters the life of you or someone you love, and you stay mad at them or yourself for an extended period of time, it will debilitate your ability to love.

Learning the importance of getting unstuck from anger can be best described by the founder of the commonly used principles of Dr. Beck's Cognitive Therapy. Cognitive therapy is all about the power that our mental thoughts have on us as a person. When there is a consistent amount of anger related discourse, it begins to give us a permanent negative distortion of the person we are angry with. In Dr. Beck's book Love is Never Enough he helps us understand that:

> "As heated arguments lead partners to withdraw
> from each other, their loving feelings seem to

wane. This phenomenon results from the fact that negative attitudes generate negative emotions, such as resentment or sadness, whereas positive attitudes generate positive emotions, such as love or happiness. When attitudes change from positive to negative, the feelings change in the same direction.

But by cutting the roots of their hostility, or at least controlling its expression, many husbands and wives are able to switch their image of each other back from negative to positive. I have often been surprised to see the return of affectionate feelings and love that had seemed totally extinguished by the intensity of the partners' hostility" (Beck, 1988, p. 333)

This is what it looks like for the state of anger to have a debilitating impact on your relationship. Our expression and even mere thought process of anger towards another person put us in a place of creating an exaggerated and often unrealistic image of the other person, and we begin to treat them in connection with our thoughts about this created figment. Dr. Beck didn't write from a Christian perspective, but I believe that some of these principles are very much centered from the life Jesus wants for us. God knows that our heart and minds are greatly linked. Proverbs was written well before Dr. Beck's grand discovery of Cognitive therapy and we have an example in chapter 4:23 that "above all else, guard your heart, for everything you do flows from it". Anger and hostility that shifts into a lifestyle will influence the way you treat others and live out your life.

Is anger a part of the healing process? In most cases, yes, but does anger have the potential to define everything that happens next? Well, yes to that as well. When we get stuck in a state of anger, it's hard to go any further. Extended anger keeps us from rest, from peace, and puts wedges on any course of redemption and love. It is essential for us all to remember that anger can be part of the process, but not the end game. I will add that there is a bit of secularity in us believing that we have a right to be angry. I love how Dallas Willard says: "nothing done through anger can be done better without it" (Wallard, 1998). That saying has helped my husband and I remember that while we do feel angry in our life, Jesus teaches us a different way to deal with that emotion.

The line I used to turn my anger into something productive for my marriage years ago was repeating "Do I love him more than I hate what he did?", and he had to ask himself the same when I made decisions that let our marriage down. Anger makes us hate the person instead of the sin, and when we are at this stage inwardly we do the same thing to ourselves, we begin hating us as a person instead of the sin in me. To cycle out of anger you have to do the hard work of separating sin from the person, and that includes you.

Hate the storm, not the person.
Hate the situation, not the person.
Hate the sin, not the person.
You were rescued because Jesus saw sin in you, not that you are the sin.

Bargaining

When bargaining symptoms begin to rise, you cycle in and out with thoughts of doing anything you can to avoid any more grief. You try and look for ways and long for everything to just go back to normal. You are almost tired and exhausted of going through this turmoil and long for it to be over as quickly as possible. You even tell the people you have hurt they can have anything they want, you are just done fighting at this point. You get to the place where you are tired of the guilt and shame you feel. You look for ways to get out, because the healing process is hard, and you try to debate whether it is even worth the fight. You may make promises to other people and to God at this stage. "I promise I won't ever drink again if you just make this go away." Often, bargaining is a seasonal symptom that tries to help you cope with the anger, you can even be caught using bargaining to try and subdue the anger with your loved ones. Here are a few bargaining tactics I've seen pop up in couples:

Becoming a doormat. If you are a peacemaker (which every couple tends to have one) becoming a doormat and doing anything that is asked of you can be an avenue of bargaining. Doormats just want all the fighting to stop. This isn't a state of healing in the relationship, it's just an attempt at bargaining "what do I need to do to make things right". Peacemakers are most at risk of becoming doormats mostly because they struggle with the tension in the room. They just want everything to stop. They feel out of control and can even get to the point where they give in or admit to something they disagree with just so the argument and fighting can be over.

In this state, if one spouse demands a public confession announced to the family – the other will give it; if one spouse demands we move on and never speak about this again – the other will listen. When one spouse is making demands, and the other spouse is postured in a position of just obedience (even decisions that take away their sense of self-respect), we are bargaining with a doormat. They will fall on the sword if needed and do whatever is asked of them to speed up the end of this uncomfortable and miserable pain of fighting. Creating a doormat may ease the tension, but this is not how we find love through the storm in our homes.

Compensating for sins. When dealing with sin, compensation is another form of bargaining where someone wants to reconcile what's been done wrong, by doing something that seems right. Behaviorally we did something we aren't proud of, so we try and find a way to behaviorally make up for it.

Working at a church, I saw people going through this season of bargaining in their personal lives as they would check every box on the Connection Card on Sunday morning. They were ready to sign up for every small group and every volunteer opportunity. Their follow through was mostly slim, but their heart was in a state of wanting to do a million things right so they could even the tally to all they've done wrong.

Accepting partial truths. Misplaced acceptance is sweeping under the rug real issues that need to be surfaced, accepted, and dealt with appropriately. It believes that the root issue is something other than the root issue. I've watched couples in my counseling office talk for months about one specific affair, and then later uncover that several affairs took place and the other spouse had their own list of unfaithfulness. We spent months talking about accepting and gaining healing on one reality when there was so much more that needed healing from.

Misplaced acceptance is my term for a temporary relief from pain. It is bargaining with the truth you feel most comfortable admitting to, so you don't have to accept and find forgiveness from it all. The spouse that was hurt can also be at risk in misplaced acceptance if they keep hidden their own personal secrets that have harmed the marriage. The voice of misplaced acceptance wants each spouse to bargain your happiness with you. This voice wants you to believe you can't get freedom from all your sin and will tell you not to acknowledge it all (that is a lie). On the path to acceptance, we are on a path to freedom, and some voices will try to get in the way of that.

What you deserve right now. I hear spouses with exposed shame say all the time "this is what I deserve" and spouses that love to remind one another that "this is better than what you deserve". The "deserve" battle is a bargaining tactic that is not in line with the Gospel. The Gospel message reminds us that we ALL deserve death, but that Christ paid that penalty for our sins. Our minds need to get out of the instinctual response of what you think you "deserve" or what your spouse "deserves" right now.

This part of accepting the storm can feel like a dry desert with no way out. Longing for happiness seems so distant, and a moment of peace can look like a sip of cold water in the midst of the blazing hot sun. The voices of bargaining in your mind will play tricks on you. These voices will tell you that healing can be found through

Becoming a Door Mat, Compensating for sins, Accepting only partial truths, or living a criminals life with What you deserve right now. Those voices are just a sip of water in a dry desert giving you false promises bargaining for freedom. Meant only to offer temporary relief in the pain your marriage is suffering right now.

Remember that our goal is not only a sip of water, our goal is also healing and freedom!

The voice of bargaining is only offering you a sip of water. The life you are striving for in your marriage does not come from a limited well but from asking Jesus to enter into your marriage and allowing him to be the peacemaker. Only Jesus has the power to bring ultimate healing, not through bargaining or compensating, but through offering us the promise that "whoever drinks the water I give him will never thirst. Indeed, the water I give them will become in them a spring of water welling up to eternal life" (John 4:14). That's the voice we need to be listening to. Jesus doesn't have representative angel attorneys that give you options to bargain as a plea for your life. Your life was meant for abundant joy and overflowing peace. Don't negotiate for anything less than what has been ransomed for your life.

You can continually try to make the pain go away through begging for this to disappear, and hiding that this ever occurred, or even running as far away from facing this disaster as you can. But no amount of compensation or doing immaculate deeds will be able to fully cover your sin. No amount of "if you do this, then I will do that" negotiating and bargaining statements will provide the healing you both ultimately need. It may have given you temporary satisfaction to breathe in your lungs and express the hurt your body feels or the pain you long to go away, but this isn't where healing is found. Freedom will come, but healing from this storm won't happen in a place of bargaining for it. Grace will win you both over. You will hear more about this later on, but a quick foreshadow is the fact that grace is given not earned, a beautiful, mind-boggling notion that most of us don't fully understand.

Depression

Depression usually comes after we get exhausted or talk ourselves out of being angry. We are just sad. The sadness about everything almost seems overwhelming, and instead of thinking about everything one box at a time, everything feels lumped together. Sadness is quickly linked with feelings of hopelessness where this is now your life. Depression puts us in a place where we accept our situation as hopeless. We aren't yet in the state of acceptance we are aiming for, instead, through depression, we are stuck feeling like this moment is as good as it is ever going to get. There are a lot of always and never sentences said in your head at this point. "I'm never going to be happy again", "I'm always going to feel like this", and "nothing is ever going to change".

Depression used to be a word that was barely understood, and I believe its insertion into our vocabulary today is still widely misunderstood. It has gone from a place of rarely being used 30-years ago to almost being over-used today. When someone says they are depressed, we don't know how to respond because we don't know what they mean. Depression is one of those words similar to love. Our culture uses the one-word "love" to describe all different forms of love. There is brotherly love, a friendship love, an intimate love, and a parental love. There are many forms of love, but when we say "I love you" or "I love this song" we are supposed to assume what type of love the person is talking about. Depression has the same kind of miscommunication. We use one word when it has many different meanings and looks different depending on the individual. We even use a comparison to decide if we are depressed. If my feelings seem different than the way my friend experiences depression, I may not think of it as depression.

Some examples of this include anxiety. Anxiety and depression seem to have a significant correspondence in our observations of depression, but that doesn't mean it is present in every situation. Extreme fatigue is another one, there is an assumption that if you are somber but are still able to get up and go to work every day you can't be depressed. There is a belief that depression is always linked with hopelessness that makes you bed-ridden. You would be surprised at how many barely, yet fully-functioning depressed people surround you in your workplace. They are everywhere. It's an emotion people are still afraid to talk about because they don't understand it. Depression is viewed as weak, and we are experts at hiding weakness.

When psychologists diagnose someone with depression or some other form of mental illness it's important for you to understand that we have a list of symptomology that will aid us with a particular diagnosis if the individual is experiencing 3 of the 6 listed symptoms over the course of a particular timeline, or some fashion of this form (Association, 2013). We categorize like this with the understanding that mental illness does not have the exact replicable features in every person that experiences it. Much like a medical professional understands that individuals have differing levels of pain tolerance. Two individuals may have the same medical condition yet have similar but different experiences of it.

When people come into a counseling office saying they are depressed they are almost caught off guard when our first question to them is "what does your depression look like to you?" or "what are some of the feelings or experiences you have that make you feel depressed?". We ask this because everyone has a different description of what depression looks like and feels like and as a counselor, you don't want to assume that your definition is the same as theirs. It differs in expression from person to person, but its results tend to be the same.

When you get tired of being angry, and no energy or collateral left to bargain with, there is just sadness and fear. When you are hopeless, the future has nothing in it you look forward to. How will I ever be happy again? Am I even allowed to be happy? Lots of questions go through your brain during a state of depression, and you don't have the energy or the motivation to seek out any answers, you just ask lots of depressing questions about how awful your life is.

Depression immobilizes you and gives the illusion of being stuck in quicksand where you don't notice the escape rope laying right beside you. There is hope, you are just struggling to see it. Don't stop looking, because I can tell you with certainty, that you won't find what you've stopped searching for. Gaining hope during a state of depression is the best way out. This is where your local church and the people around you can be your biggest influencers, with the single gift of hope. (And if your church home doesn't offer you hope, you should consider

> *Journal:* Depression robs me from experiencing any form of joy. I sit in public settings, just looking like a girl typing on her computer, but no one sees my pain, the desperation of my heart at this moment, at the tearing of my skin from my body. I sip my coffee and cycle through Psalm 38 feeling that David's words depict the cries of my heart: *"Lord, do not rebuke me in your anger or discipline me in your wrath. Your arrows have pierced me, and your hand has come down on me. Because of your wrath there is no health in my body; there is no soundness in my bones because of my sin. My guilt has overwhelmed me like a burden too heavy to bear. (1-4)"*

surrounding yourself around a group of people that are aiming to be the hands and feet and Jesus and sit at the table with you during this storm.)

Getting out of depression is a hard chore to do. You really have to get to a point where you start telling your body and mind what to do instead of letting the depression tell you how to live. What we need to do is get up and get dressed in the morning, even if you have nowhere to go. Take a shower, take a walk, or sit at a different coffee shop every day, you might even see me there.

Dating God through Depression

There are many people I know, and many people my social media accounts remind me are in my life but not all of them I have a personal relationship with. The coffee shop I am at today has 8 groups of people around me that all coordinated with someone else in their life to meet at this exact spot today. They are looking at each other in the eye. Their phones are out of sight, and they are engaging with one another. They are connecting, sharing, bonding, laughing, praying, and developing something special with each other. This is what God wants from us, to not just be another friend on our friend list but to be an intimate encounter and unique relationship in your life. Meet with Him, laugh with Him, develop, and share with Him. Have experiences and places with Him that are special to the two of you, places where you feel known, and places you pursue knowing Him.

We need to get out of this depression, we can't stay in this place. If misery loves company, let's assume hope loves hopeful company as well. Dating God and finding rest in His word will provide the faith we need to catapult out of this depressed state and into acceptance. You may not feel much power at this point if you are still feeling distanced from God, but it will come, and the words of His pages will rejuvenate the strength in your bones. Even when your relationship with God isn't where you want it to be, or where He desires it to be, don't give up on dating just yet.

Dating God is just another term for personalizing your faith and spending time with your Maker, your love. You may have grown up hearing it called having a "quiet time", but that sounds like a boring relationship to me. I have never asked Matt to have a quiet time with me. I have asked him to spend "quality time" with me, but never quiet time. And honestly, where would we find quiet time in this house with little monkeys everywhere. My husband and I are always in a relationship, but dating each other means we make time for one another. It means we put a value on our relationship and prioritize it in our busy lives. Dating gives a reminder at the "us" we are striving for beyond the "us" that simply passes each other every day. Our relationship with God deems more than a "quiet time", it is making consistent dates to break from the world and focus on just us and having special time together, and even special places can help grow your relationship with God.

Special places, spots, and things. I have counseled someone through an emotional breakup where one of the things the two of them agreed on together was that they wouldn't go to 'Trivia Night' with anyone else if they dated someone new. They declared 'Trivia Night' as a special place that defined and shaped their relationship, and they wanted that spot to belong to their memories as being

> *Journal: There is a particular coffee shop that feels safe to me. It's a 25-minute drive but I know that the chances of someone I know walking in are pretty slim. I stay there for hours so I just wait until the comfy chairs are available so I can plop my butt down, breathe, and hear what God has for me that day. God is helping me through this depression by dating me right now. Strange concept I know, but so true. When I lie awake at 2:00 in the morning struggling to fall back asleep with my brain spinning through the last couple months I try and turn my attention to prayer, and ask God which coffee shop he wants to take me to the next day. I ask him to meet me there, and I even ask him to save me a seat in one of the comfy chairs. He is with me, even in my sadness, even when the world feels darker to me, even when my surroundings don't seem like they make sense. Dating God through this storm has birthed the sweetest fruit in this restless soul.*

special. Sounds trivial if you are looking from the outside but if you catch a glimpse of their heart, they remember the connection they formed on that regular night and experience during the week. A dating space for them that meant more than just trivia.

Coffee shops have been my special place during my most recent difficult season of life, and I have had other seasons where God and I dated at the gym or every day when my feet hit the concrete running.

Where is He meeting you at this point in your life? If you can't come up with an answer, it's time for you two to find "your spot".

In finding healing even during a depression, gain identified spots, places, and moments that will become the special things that you and God connected through as He sat with you through this storm. A special chair where you sat and read that book that challenged your faith. That blanket you used to cover yourself for safety as you sought comfort in the scary world in front of you. A cup of coffee that started each day as a reminder that it is a new day. Or even a place at the table that became your chair of surrender, when you sat there on your darkest moments, and it reminded you to give it all away, to gain courage through gaining faith.

/ / Exercise: Find External Sources for Hope / /

Another great place to start is with music. Listening to depressing music is only going to help you stay depressed. Listening to songs of hope when you feel hopeless will give you power and bring back energy to your soul little by little.

Music is a valuable tool used in my house, we tend to encourage each other with songs anytime we go through something difficult. Matt is a drummer so music is the language he speaks and he happens to have a gift of sending people a song that connects with what they are going through. As you find outside noises to intercede hope in your life, we put together a collection of songs that have served as hope for us and the hopeful comfort to get you started finding external means of hope outside yourself as you learn to gain it for yourself.

Lyrics feel like a love letter, and God's Word will feel even more personal while overcoming pain in your life. When strength regains in my body after a storm, I love that God and I had distinct meeting spots through some of the hardest days of my life that I can look back on.

Acceptance

Here we are, but the path to acceptance is no easy road. Your whole time reading this I have led up to this stage calling it trying to reach the goal of getting to Acceptance. Now that you are here I want to change it up. You weren't ready to hear this at the beginning of this chapter because we were still stuck feeling hopeless. Acceptance was easier to grab onto, so I used that word to help get you started. This path has been more than just about acceptance. As we move through the symptoms we mentioned, and even some we didn't get to mention, can I nudge you to believe that this is a path to something more, more than just acceptance? This has actually been a path to hope. Not a path to answers, not a path to everything's better, not a path to solutions, it has been a path to feeling hope, even if just a little. When we start out feeling hopeless, the real journey is finding hope in the hopeless circumstances. Hope through our feelings, hope when the odds are against us and hope when nothing seems possible. The real path we have been on is a journey to finding and feeling…Hope.

When we are depressed, we feel hopeless, and even though we have been working towards accepting our awful circumstances, acceptance without hope just looks like depression. If acceptance without hope manifests into depression, then acceptance with hope can manifest into the faith we need to get through a storm in our life.

We still don't have all the answers, we still aren't sure what next looks like, but we get to a lifestyle of hope when we just believe that there is a next, that there is an after that has meaning from this storm. For some of you, getting to the point where you begin to see a tomorrow is a huge step in recovery. We get to this place where we acknowledge that sin did happen but there is more that can happen next. As we move from a small glimmer of hope into developing a lifestyle of faith, God will do the work in our life that only He can do as we humbly position ourselves before Him.

With hope, you begin to see the fog lifting and can start to wrap your brain around what to do with this new story that's been written within your marriage. As the fog lifts, here is where you decide if you want this to be the middle or the end of your story, and where you begin to believe that you and your marriage can be more than this awful story. You accept the ugly parts of who you are and what has been brought into your marriage and begin to gain an ounce of energy that says you don't want to live your life in the pain of your sin or theirs forever.

Finding hope from this awful storm in your marriage is a part of your story, but it doesn't mean it has to be the end page for your marriage. What starts as hope can develop into freedom as we continue on. Even if freedom still doesn't seem possible, at this place, hope is a huge accomplishment. If all you have today is merely a desire for freedom without fully being able to feel it, I am okay with that, and I will celebrate that as a forward step along this journey. We can believe in and feel the freedom later even if I would love for you to feel it now. Beliefs can be ignited with a single desire, so a desire for freedom is a great place to start on the road ahead.

Step IV
CLEANSING AFTER THE STORM

I hate the process of cleaning. I love to see things spotless, shiny, and new. But the path getting there isn't any fun. It's not fun when I do the dishes, when I do the laundry, when I organize my finances, when I mow the yard. The process isn't fun for me. But the cleansing period is worth the end result. We're moving forward not because things look pretty right now, but because we have hope that something spotless, shiny, and made new is up ahead for our lives, and for our marriage.

Chapter 8
Being Stripped

Do you remember how many times you fell down as a kid? It is limitless. Your wobbly body was stretching and growing, and you were utterly careless at tripping over cracks in the sidewalks, curbs that creep up on you, and those reckless double-dog-dares that were asking for a scrape on the knee and a broken arm. Band-Aids are a necessity in a house full of kids for daily moments like these.

We just can't have enough Band-Aids in our house, we are continually running out. And of course, if you're going to sport a Band-Aid on your body, it needs to be themed. Star Wars, or a superhero, or a princess one for our little girl. Our kids went through a lot of pain to earn that Band-Aid and they want something, including a story, to go with it.

Two pains take place before you get a Band-Aid: the first is the actual act of hurt being caused to your body; the second is when your Mom pulls out the peroxide to drip over the open wound to clean it. AHHHH!! My kids would rather hide an injury than have me pour that stuff on their body. I don't blame them, I remember that feeling. I remember being told how cool it is, and I use that trick on my kids too. "Watch how neat it is to see the bubbles foam up as it cleans your body."

What's really happened is that the flesh on our skin has broken open, and now we are told we have to go through another amount of pain before we get the reward of our favorite themed Band-Aid. As a kid, and even as adults, we want the story that comes with the scar but forget that there is a cleansing that comes first. The Band-Aid doesn't happen before the peroxide gets poured on the wound to clean it up. If we skip the step of the painful peroxide, we can try to heal the wound but gain an infection. That's not healing.

When we get to the place of accepting the nature of our sin, we feel it, we see it, and we have to go to the medicine cabinet, make that petrifying look on our face and get ready to pour the peroxide on the wound. How this peroxide metaphor looks for us emotionally, is that we feel the weight of disappointment we have caused those around us. We watch the hurtful bubbles foam up at the top, and we keep pouring it on until little by little there are no more bubbles, which means the wound is clean.

In a sense, we have to do more than just know the pain we caused others, we begin to feel it, and it stings. Empathy gives us a window into understanding, and it's time to try to understand. It's time to do something with our understanding. Time to pour the peroxide on our soul, watch the bubbles pop-up and expect the healing to do its work. As we have been doing assessments, noticing our emotions, and recognizing ownership, it is time to do something with the sin and weaknesses we have identified within us.

Sin is not just an action, not just a behavior, sin is any presence in our life of putting ourselves before our Creator. We can do this in many ways, and even multiple times in our day, and the more we recognize our faults and shortcomings in our sin, the more the flesh from our bodies becomes stripped. I am convinced that when we ask Jesus into our hearts and lives, that the transformation that comes next is one of the influences of the world slowly being stripped from our bodies as He refines us and makes us His. The Holy Spirit tends to do its work at pouring a spiritual peroxide all over our flesh.

We can hear the beauty in being cleansed and renewed without fully understanding the process it takes to be made new in Christ and begin to truly mirror His heart and character in the way we live out our everyday lives. In every growth opportunity we face, some small and some major, we go through a transformation. In the middle of the storm, it is hard to see any refining take place. In the middle of the storm, all we feel is the pain of scraping off the scabs from our skin. Without the hope that our scabs can be healed, all we see are scars that feel attached to our bodies forever.

This is what the stripping process is like: before we heal, we go through a process of feeling. We are slowly ridding our hearts and minds, and souls of everything that is not pleasing to the Lord until all we are left with is open arms. We seem to get to that "rock bottom" moment people talk about where we humbly stand before God, fall to our knees, and speak with the words of "take it all Lord but give me Jesus". It's a period of our life where we come back to our Father and remember that He is all we need, and it is often in the storm seasons of our life where we realize that He is actually ALL we have.

Everything else in our life is fleeting; everything else in our life has a date of expiration. He becomes our constant and our only consistency. Through a period of cleansing, we go from rock bottom to a full understanding of what it means for Jesus to be our Rock. That whatever we have turned to and found a false hope in, is nothing compared to falling back in love and being in awe of our need solely for our Creator. Being stripped can be a painful process, but one that God can turn into something beautiful.

Humility and Submission

Even though pain can be no fun, don't minimize the importance of trusting your Father to strip the world from you. He has a plan, and even more than that He gives us instruction on our way out of a storm.

In the Bible, James is a short book that is packed with God's truth. In chapter 4 he gives a depiction of calling us an "adulterous people", which is what we are when we are children of God and disobey His instruction in our lives. There is a war between Spirit and Flesh within us and any time we fall into the trap of choosing the flesh, James tells us that we become friends with the world, and "friendship with the world means enmity against God" (James 4:4). But he doesn't stop there, he goes on in verse 6 to say: "But He has given us more grace...".

"More Grace", what an amazing concept we need to impress on

our hearts. How undeserving we are of just Grace alone. Our jealous God wants all our attention, love, and devotion to turn to Him, but instead, He sees us fall short of the obedience He deserves, and He somehow gives us "more grace". Grace in itself given by our Father is such a beautiful thing that the phrase "MORE grace" my mind cannot even fathom. We sit in awe of this undeserving place we are in and get to a point where the only way out of this storm is turning back to our God and sitting in submission before Him. James knew this and in the following verses 7-10 he jumps into instruction on how we turn back to our Father in submission.

> "Submit yourselves, then, to God. Resist the devil, and he will flee from you. Come near to God, and he will come near to you. Wash your hands, you sinners, and purify your hearts, you double-minded. Grieve, mourn, and wail. Change your laughter to mourning and your joy to gloom. Humble yourselves before the Lord, and He will lift you up." (James 4:7-10)

Submission to our Father plays a significant role in the spiritual peroxide of the stripping process in humbling ourselves before God. Humility before our Father is what we must do as we seek to heal the other relationships in our life that have been impacted by this storm. Sins presence needs cleansing and James helps us turn towards our Father as he answers the "how do we do this" question that is swirling through our head after a storm.

As you sit in confusion not knowing what to do next and scrolling the internet for self-help tips for your life, God gives us the steps we need. James lines it out for us in this scripture, but for all my checklist readers out there (which I am one of), let me put James 4:7-10 into a step-by-step list to help us with a clear direction:

1. Submit yourselves back to God.
2. Turn away from the friendship we made with the devil and the earthly flesh within our sin.
3. Seek out God. Read, fast, pray. Take action steps to get closer to him, and he will come near to you.
4. Now that you have God near you, you have His strength with you to help you get clean, to purify your heart and your mind.
5. Grieve, mourn, and wail. As you gain a cleansed spirit, you will grieve as you fully start to grasp your disobedience and His faithful love.
6. You will go through a season where your happiness turns into mourning and joy goes through a period of gloom.
7. In doing these things you will become stripped, and through the stripping process you will be humbling yourself before the Lord, but He has a plan to lift you up.

Don't miss this. James gives us these small tips that will bear a tremendous amount of fruit in your life. Let's sit here for a bit to make sure we get it.

Can you imagine this list if it ended with the sadness of step 6 (joy turned to mourning and gloom)? Can you even fathom right now having your entire life in a stuck season of mourning and gloom? Do you understand that it could have ended right there? But it doesn't, and praise God that there is more!

In our disobedience, the punishment for sin is death so it would have made perfect sense here that on our path back to God we could very well end with sorrow, regret, and suffering. It doesn't stop there though, and the hope in step 7 that the Lord will lift us up means that we have to trust Him. It tells us

> *Journal: I am relying on God to give me a hopeful ending to this pain. I want to be lifted up in a way I don't understand or deserve. I know I cannot live my whole life feeling the way I do in this moment.*

that all of these steps are hard, but if we do them right, will have a step 7 hopeful ending to them.

I know you are with me, here in this place of hating the sin within you and wishing for a heart transplant that could be a one-day procedure to cure your broken and fragile soul. This will be a process, a journey, not a one-day procedure. Each of these steps in James is given a numerical value because I believe they were meant in that order, and each step needs its own amount of time.

In a world that seeks answers, James gives us clear direction from what God is expecting next in your life to help you get unstuck from this storm. Let's look through these verses again, and reflect on the order. Does everything on our numerical healing list look like it's in the right place?

My initial thoughts are to think that step 3 (seek God) and step 4 (purify your heart and mind) would be switched. We want to get our lives back on track and become cleansed and purified in our heart and mind before we do the "come near to God, and He will come near to you". That may be what we initially think, but God and James are both way smarter than that, they know that we need the Spirit of God to help us through the cleansing, not the other way around. If we could do this on our own, we wouldn't need a Savior from the world to begin with. Jesus reminds us in John 15:5 that "I am the vine; you are the branches. If you remain in me and I in you, you will bear much fruit; apart from me you can do nothing." We need to come near to God before we get clean so that He can do the cleansing, so that He can prepare us to be a branch that comes back to life and bear sweet fruit. Apart from God, we cannot do this crucial step.

Many people live their lives reversing numbers 3 and 4, and they end up doing a disservice to themselves and their relationship with God because they don't realize they need God's help to do step 4 and work on cleansing. These are the people (you may need to admit if you are one of them) who want to get their life and themselves together and perfect before they go back to church. People that may be having trouble even praying to God in repentance of their sin because they want to get themselves to a place where He will be proud of them first – then they will feel better to pray to Him.

It's actually the other way around, try and follow along with this one - you need to draw close to God right where you are so that He can help you be the you that you are trying to be on your own. The only thing He asks of you is to work at resisting the devil, to stop the sin and the disobedience you recognize within you. At this point, even acknowledging that you see your sin and want to get out of it says a lot. Then draw near to Him, because you are going to need Him close to do the rest.

God as Father

Our God is the perfect model of a parent. The hardest thing for me to do is to watch my children suffer in any form. I would take away their suffering in an instant and if there were a way to protect them from any type of emotional harm or future storms I would do it, but I know that I would also be doing them a disservice by taking away these precious moments of growth. Growth comes through the sufferings we endure. Even physically, there are growing pains as the body hurts and aches as it stretches and grows. Watching your kids get picked on at school and learning the pain of the world is hard to do. Watching them get punished at home for disobeying their Dad and I is not fun for us, but we know that they will learn lessons better from a blend of grace and consequence than our protection of making it all go away.

God, our Father, parents us utilizing every opportunity He can to continue writing His story on our lives. He does not waste, and the mess you feel stuck in today He will strip you of so that this moment goes from defining our lives to transforming our hearts. That is what makes Him the ultimate parent!

The parent I sometimes view when I look at heaven is a God that is pointing His finger at me and saying, "You put yourself in this situation, Emily, now try and get yourself out" (sounds a lot like one of those Bargaining tactics). That's not my Father. And when I get rid of that negative voice in my head, I hear a Father that is disappointed in His daughter at times, but one that is saying, "Do you trust me to take care of you through this, even though it may hurt?" and "Will you let me be Lord, and make something beautiful out of these shattered pieces?" He loves me more than I comprehend. He loves you too. No matter your situation, God does not leave you there. Come near to Him, and He will lift you up. Watching our children suffer is a hard task to do, but we never leave them in that spot, and your God won't leave you either. He will do something through the storm, He will help this pain have a purpose, He always does.

We were crafted towards healing, and this pain has a remedy. It is almost like being at the doctor's office as a kid and hearing the doctor, the nurses, and your trusted parents trying to explain to you the benefits of getting a shot. "This is going to hurt a bit, but it's going to help you." That doesn't make sense? Hurt and help don't go together, they are separate things. Hurt means pain, and pain means bad! Here you are in a tiny room with an adult holding a long needle that your brain magnifies to being 10 times larger than it actually is and they tell you to "relax". Again...makes no sense? How do you relax for a pain you know is coming? The safe and trusted adults even count to let you know when to expect it, they say 1...2, and they push the shot in on 2 so you don't tense up on the 3, how sneaky.

The child in me hears the voice of my Father as I wrestle with the existence of sin's tug on my life. There have been many painful moments of dealing with my own sin and shame; different areas of loss and circumstances not turning out the way I would want them to. They

> *Journal: But I trust you Lord. I trust that this long needle is going to do something good for the sickness I have in my body called sin. That you can cover this, and that you are bigger. That you will turn this from being about me, into pointing completely to bringing you glory.*

are all painful times and memories in my life that were no fun, and I wish never to repeat. Some of the most painful ones I wish could completely be erased. I wish at times I could make even the small triggers in my life that remind me of these events go away. On the flip side, of all of these, I can see the transformation that took place as God grew this girl through the most painful times in her life. Right now, I have learned enough and have gone through enough to know that the experience we endure facing sin's ugly face head-on is painful – but there is power in taking it to the cross.

God is for us

There is an exhilaration in becoming a Christian, and an innocent expectation that life is going to get easier, but the more we become aware of God's love for us, the more we recognize how we fall short in our disobedience to our faithful Father. Our humility increases as we see more and more the full extent of our everyday unfaithfulness to Him, and as you start to see out of the fog and see broken pieces from this storm that are yours to own, know that God is still right there with you. Being stripped is a process that goes through many different stages and steps, but what will stay consistent every time, is that God can heal, God is a redeemer, and He's got you.

When we make the bold step to turn towards God, we then get to hold the power and the peace that He is with us and take that truth on every step of this healing

> *Journal: I keep forgetting that truth, that God is for my marriage; that He is with us through the storm we are going through. I will have a good evening where I am feeling positive and feeling like I am on my way out of this storm, and then I will have three bad days in a row, where my whole body feels like mush. So many things are triggering me into a setback. Being stripped for me has been a constant reminder of all that feels lost. But I must fight with the reminder that God does not leave me here, that much is to come that I can't yet see.*

journey we are on. Our God is not waiting for you at the end of this painful tunnel, His arms are open now, right in the middle of the storm. He will walk with you even in the desert. Don't wait to turn to your Father once you feel the storm is over. Your transformation will happen with God walking out of the storm with you, not in Him waiting for you at the end.

Remember that we need Him as we walk through what is up ahead. Begin to feel Him holding you in His arms and sense His Spirit doing CPR on your soul as you are brought back to life. Let this start with you and then let His Spirit perform a miracle in your marriage that we need His help to do.

Child of God

Examine your life, what has been stripped and taken away because of sin? Is your joy gone? Have you lost esteem in yourself? Are you feeling a disconnection with God? Do you miss the friend you had in your spouse, the spouse that now looks at you like an enemy? Have you lost your integrity? Respect for yourself? Have you lost hope?

Journal. Life without margin isn't living…it is a slow suffocation until you collapse. The jobs I had became my identity that had given me purpose and life to a degree that was unhealthy. I am now having to recognize that the only foundation I have is my title as a child of God. I can rebuild those other titles, but this time I need to do it with my identity rooted foundationally in being a child of God. It's the only thing to cling to when we have nothing left. The past few months I have been pretty lousy at everything, every title I had has suffered, wife, mom, leader, counselor, etc… When our priorities in life get off track we become more susceptible to sin, and when we make the choice into sin it will have an impact on your whole life. To get back on track, we have to finish the pain to find the healing, remembering that God is with us.

Of all the voices putting you down, there is one voice, and one title that you haven't lost. With everything you both may feel right now, what remains constant both in the storm and on the brightest of days, is that you are a child of God. Nothing can change your adoption papers. In the cleansing part of your healing, some of your other titles may have gotten lost or distorted – your job, your position, sense of self, etc... Think of the story being written on your life, start to see that we are beginning a new chapter, the story that is unfolding is finding meaning in the only title that matters in your life - being a child of God. And when being a child of God is the only title you have that is constant, we learn to shape everything we do in our life from that title. God is for us, and once we reach this point, then God can parent us through the difficult stages to come.

Journal: I'm almost on house arrest right now. No one has told me I need to stay home and sort through my junk, I am just sitting here, every day, reflecting on how to get my life back on track, and how it got off the rails to begin with. I can't seem to get unstuck from the moments of guilt and shame defining my life. I am self-punishing and if I am not careful I could declare myself to have a life sentence.

Feeling the Disappointment

Are you allowing yourself to feel? I know this process has been hard, grueling, and painful beyond compare for you. I believe you didn't walk into sin because your life was going smoothly at the time. There were hurts and pains that you were experiencing that made you sensitive to sin's lure, but through this process, you need to have moments where you separate from how all this is affecting you, and feel the disappointment you have caused so many others. They are hurt, and the pain they feel they have to wrestle with because of decisions they didn't even make. Feeling their pain will only encourage us to never want to experience all of this again, but it's not easy.

If we are honest with their disappointment, people are only disappointed in people they expected more and better from. Strangely, they are disappointed because they love us and feel helpless watching and hearing what has happened. The position we put others in to deal with a new storm narrative is hard on them more than you may realize. You would hope to never be in their situation, so don't take lightly the position you may have put others in after walking into this storm. You may notice yourself feeling the disappointment of others, but we need to balance their pain without latching it on to your identity. When the suffering of others and the blame you feel within yourself attaches to your identity, this will begin the cycle of shame and guilt that will try and take over your life.

Shame and Guilt

When guilt defines your life, you feel worthless, and when shame latches on to your leg like a leech at the lake, it sucks you dry of anything positive or good. Your life becomes egocentric with your guilt in the center of all you do. "I can't have fun right now, I don't deserve it"; "I can't be happy, I have done nothing to earn it". Without a fight, the mental list of what you deserve and need to earn will go on and on and will consume your life with the usual things you now feel you need permission to do. Guilt and shame require there own process of being stripped from your identity right now.

The guilt cycle will try and run your life. It will feed you lies and hopes you forget what truth says. Truth says that before your confession and even before, during, and after your regretful actions you start and end every day with worth. Guilt will make you feel worthless and will have you lose sight of the truth that you have worth.

Shame will keep us stuck. Feeling like there is a rain cloud following us everywhere we go. "You aren't allowed to feel happy" is the whisper it brings to your ear. "You aren't allowed to experience the warmth of the sun", you are in your own prison without recognizing the door to this cage is unlocked. Step out of shame.

The guilt and shame cycle will put you into a deeper pit or will strengthen your identity as you realize that nothing, nothing, I am going to repeat it, nothing, can take away your title as a child of God.

Even the worst actions and the wandering astray of the prodigal son did not waver the excitement of his father to watch his son return (Luke 15:11-32). Proud or disgusted by his sons' actions made no difference in the world, he was still his son. Your Father in Heaven views you as His own, a masterpiece of His creation, a unique design crafted in His own image. There is no place for shame in that title.

A life defined by shame is not one to look forward to. In the process of being stripped of the world, we may feel these things. Feeling shame and guilt for doing something wrong is a part of being a moral human being, but staying in that state is denying your identity and what Jesus did for you on the cross.

At this point, I know you would love to hear me say: "neither do I condemn you, go now and leave your life of sin" (John 8:11). The longing to hear that comes from your hope to gain permission from me to get out of the trap you are in. My friend, I have no merit and no sense of authority in your life to give you that freedom, but, Jesus has the power to speak those words to you. These words are being written out to point you to the God that saves and the Jesus that knew you needed a Savior and a path into freedom before you ever knew you needed it.

There is power in the Gospel. Our God brings things back to life. Jesus is a heart doctor, and He examines the heart of those He loves. Feeling remorseful for the ugly parts of your life shows the intent of your heart and displays that transformation is at work. As with each step of this process, they are all a part of the process, the danger comes when they enter your life and become a part of your identity. When any of these steps control your mind or debilitate your life, that's when they are unhealthy. For now, acknowledging that you are wearing a stained shirt is essential to realizing we need a plan on how to clean it.

Let me follow that up with some truth that you need to hear today. What if I told you I knew I guy; a guy that would switch shirts with you. A guy that when he puts on your stained shirt, it is washed white as snow. He can wear your shirt and give it back to you whiter than you had it to begin with. You may feel everyone's disappointment right now, but before you deal with the pain that the world feels, you need to start with you and the guy I know that can get any stain out of a shirt. Really, He's a miracle worker, and it is vital for you to hear that this cleansing period is pivotal because it begins with you and Jesus. Surrender yourself back to him. Before we can deal with the weight of letting everyone down, we need to first gain strength from understanding that we let God down most of all and He needs to be where we draw near to first to gain the strength and wisdom for how to do all we have left to do. We must draw near to God as He will be the strength to direct what next looks like and what next will look like to heal the relationships in your life.

Chapter 9
David's Storm

There's someone else that went through the cleansing after the storm that we can turn to. A man from the Bible who expressed his emotions on paper for us to walk alongside and witness his experience as we connect it back to ours. Let's use this chapter to take a breath from our story and our situation and just reflect on someone from the Bible that had his fair share of experience with guilt, shame, and recovering from sin, let's see what he does with it.

If you haven't heard much about King David let me try to give you a snapshot. He wasn't the King you would expect much to be written about depending on the parts of his life you gravitate to. Our Christian culture lends itself to build up leaders that have lives full of high integrity and little shame. The Bible, however, is filled with stories of spiritual leaders that seemed unqualified, and even ones with major moments in disobedience that God still saw potential in. David was one of those leaders. Here was a guy who lived on a roller coaster of emotional and spiritual faith. We don't see a lot of consistency in his level of obedience to God. David's story makes us wonder what God was thinking putting his perfect Son Jesus in the same lineage? (I am sure there are a few people in your family tree you aren't sure how they got there either.) God knew what He was doing even if we would have organized things differently.

With the witness of David's trials, sufferings, and major growth encounters he had in his relationship with God, we are given a window into his lessons of overcoming. David went through an intense amount of time being stripped and formed by a God that wouldn't let go. The Psalms are filled with many of David's attempts to process out his life on paper. His way of processing is filled with vulnerability and pain for David but serves as a blessing for us to learn from today.

Many people and prophets spoke into David's life. The 51st Psalm is composed after the prophet Nathan had addressed David for his encounter with Bathsheba, the married woman that David not only desired, but had for himself. After Nathan's confrontation, David confesses his sin. It isn't like he was unaware of his sin at the time, but there is a power that surfaces when a sin is brought to light and no longer hidden in the darkness.

As we are all learning the extent of being stripped by God, we are finding a similar work present within us, as sins are acknowledged, recognized, and denounced, we are now in a position like David of confessing from a place you aren't proud to be standing in. We are going through our days wishing for the regrets of yesterday to be gone, but today our sins are right here before us, right here before our God and we look for what to do with it. As we stand beside David with a broken heart, and in humility before our Father, we can look at David as an example of the next steps to take in our healing with God.

It can be hard to see beauty in the moment of confession, but this aspect of weeping before God and humbling ourselves before him serves as a great example of turning back to God after living in disobedience to him. Wherever you are today, whatever you have done, whatever you feel has been done to you, know you can follow David as he turns to the Father to rescue him out from sin. David speaks to God in Psalm 51 in a way that reminds us (1) of our Father's Unfailing Love; (2) the plea for God to Cleanse Me and Don't Leave Me; (3) the declaration for God to Use My Broken Spirit; and (4) saying May it Please the Lord in the blessings of life to come.

Unfailing Love

David turns to God, once again as he has done before, and starts his Psalm like this:

Psalm 51:1-6

"Have mercy on me, Oh God, according to your unfailing love; according to your great compassion blot out my transgressions. Wash away all my iniquity and cleanse me of my sin. For I know my transgressions, and my sin is always before me. Against you, you only, have I sinned, and done what is evil in your sight; so you are right in your verdict and justified in your judge. Surely I was sinful at birth, sinful from the time my mother conceived me. Yet you desired faithfulness even in the womb; you taught me wisdom in that secret place."

David's eloquent plea to God is so raw, so honest, and so true. Filled in these verses is an example of David processing out God stripping his heart after sin. There is much we can learn through David's expression of coming back to the Father.

He starts with acknowledging who God is and recognizing the truth of God's unfailing love. How many sentences does it usually take us before we can ever start with how much He loves us when we talk to God about our weaknesses? The last thing we feel in that moment is loved, we don't deserve it is all we can think. Instead, we believe that God sees us the way everyone else seems to be treating us. It's hard to see a God filled with unfailing love when all you feel is external condemnation. Somehow David is able to start in a place that often takes us a while to get to.

Maybe he's done this before?

He reminds himself of God's unfailing love and God's power

to blot out transgression. Do you know where the ability and power come from to be able to blot out transgressions? David claims it comes from God's compassion. God's unfailing love and compassion on us are the gifts we don't realize we've been given. We have done nothing to deserve God's compassion. Your Father just loves you, no strings attached. Nothing you do and nothing that has been done to you can change God's unfailing and ever-faithful love. David starts this Psalm with God's unfailing love because he knows he still has it, he hasn't lost it because of his sin.

David shows an intimacy with God where even when they aren't in good standing he asks His Father to cleanse him. Almost inviting God to strip him of his iniquity, and understanding that the moral sin he has committed he has done foremost in subjection to his Father. David has hurt and disappointed many people in his sin, but turns to God and says, "against you, you only, have I sinned".

He doesn't stop there, in fact, he is just getting started. Next, he claims ownership. He recognizes with full assurance that he is guilty, no excuses, no sorry I was having a bad day, just guilty. Telling God that His verdict is right and He is a justified judge, no arguments there.

While God gives us an unfailing love, we tend to give him faithful disobedience. David is an example of this, and if I could put it in a smaller font, I would write and so are you and I. Almost as if I want that to be kept a secret, that you and I tend to be faithfully disobedient. David owns it, He says sin is always before him.

The Psalm is continued with the reminder that David was a sinner from the start and the understanding that God desired faithfulness from the start as well. David goes into depth that we have been failing at righteousness even from conception. A great reminder that while we currently feel stuck in our present disobedience, God had known this tension long before this instance entered our lives. David understands his God is disappointed in this, but he also realizes that he has been getting it wrong his whole life. His descriptions show us that even though he isn't the model servant or the example we necessarily want our kids to look up to, he knows his position before his Father and knows that he is undeservedly loved by Him.

Cleanse me and Don't Leave me

Psalm 51:7-12

> "Cleanse me with hyssop, and I will be clean, wash me and I will be whiter than snow. Let me hear joy and gladness; let the bones you have crushed rejoice. Hide your face from my sins and blot out all my iniquity. Create in me a pure heart, Oh God, and renew in me a steadfast spirit within me. Do not cast me from your presence or take your Holy Spirit from me. Restore to me the joy of your salvation and grant me a willing spirit, to sustain me."

David has come to his Father feeling the dirt of sin on his skin, seeing the stains on his shirt that he is ashamed of. He cries out to God knowing he is the one who can make him clean. A King. A King who can order commands to bring moments of earthly joy and clothes made for royalty. A King is seen crying out to the God most High when he is surrounded by those that would follow him. David knows that God is the only one that can cleanse his heart of the mistakes he has made. Not only does David cry out in his emotion, but he speaks to God in these verses wanting something more.

"Let me hear joy and gladness..." are David's words. Even with sadness and pain consuming him, he seeks emotions of happiness. In our cleansing period, we often get to the point where we question whether joy and gladness will be permitted in our life ever again. This is the reason I believe only a few people take the road less traveled into full repentance of sin. There is an entrapment that comes into your mind that says you won't ever be happy again. That level of hopelessness makes some people believe their only chance

113

at happiness is to stay in their sin feeling like it is the only source of comfort left in their life. This is a lie. There is hope. David knows it, he pleads for it to God: "Let the bones you have crushed rejoice". He is specific in asking God to not just forgive him, but restore him to life again. Oh, the lessons we can learn from David's heart.

David comes to God knowing he is the only one that can cleanse and renew his heart, and he turns to God asking him to not cast away the Spirit's presence from him. He gives us a reminder at the end of that section in verse 12 to "grant me a willing spirit, to sustain me". What a reminder. Not only do we need God to cleanse us, but when we turn to him in repentance, we have to do so by asking him to change our heart, and to give us a willing spirit for the days to come. He isn't just asking for forgiveness for what has happened, but for the Spirit's voice and presence to sustain him going forward. He is asking God to cleanse him, and requesting that He doesn't leave him.

Use My Broken Spirit

Psalm 51:13-17

"Then I will teach transgressors your ways, so that sinners will turn back to you. Deliver me from the guilt of bloodshed, Oh God, you who are God my Savior, and my tongue will sing of your righteousness. Open my lips Lord, and my mouth will declare your praise. You do not delight in sacrifice, or I would bring it; you do not take pleasure in burnt offerings. My sacrifice, Oh God, is a broken spirit; a broken and contrite heart you God, will not despise."

In these verses we see David talk like it is done. He speaks to God with a glimpse of the renewed heart he is asking for. "Then I will teach," he says to God. I will take what you have done for me and display your righteousness to others "so that sinners will turn back to you". How radiant an image? To be delivered from the guilt of bloodshed that justice would declare undeserved. This treatment is counterculture for sure. Nowhere on this earth can we find this level of deliverance but from God or someone with a heart like him.

Next is the declaration David makes that he would do anything, anything, to get right with his Father again. We see David going through a mental state of Bargaining on his own path to Acceptance. If it were a burnt offering, it would be done, but he knows that is not what God is after. His sacrifice is what we are relating to as we read David's words: "My sacrifice, Oh God, is a broken spirit".

This is where we are at, this is where we have come to. The process of looking within ourselves in our attempt to turn back to God has put us in this place before our Father. We have a broken spirit that feels as though life is missing from our soul. Don't wander away scared it has left you forever. We are offering our broken spirit to God believing that he can restore it back to life. I can tell you it will be a life fuller than you had realized before all this if you give it over to Him.

May It Please You

David ends with a statement of perplexing prosperity. This whole thing has been about confessing and turning back to God after sin. Why does he add these last two verses that almost seem out of place:

Psalm 51:18,19

"May it please you to prosper Zion, to build up the walls of Jerusalem. Then you will delight in the sacrifices of the righteous, in burnt offerings offered whole; then bulls will be offered on your altar."

Who in the world does David think he is at this moment that he can tell God, (my paraphrase) "and since your clearing my sins away, maybe you wouldn't mind blessing me in the process". What? I think you went a bit too far David, stretching your prayer a little over the edge there.

Or maybe not. What we see here is the confidence of a King who knows that his God hasn't left his side. A man who knows that God wants what is best for His people even when they aren't doing what is best for Him. He seeks this blessing request in verse 18 because he declares that they will have a nation that places offerings in obedience to God's altar (remember we are in the Old Testament with the atonement of sins). He asks for the blessing on Zion and the walls of Jerusalem so they can glorify God not to glorify David. His heart in this prayer is a king speaking to his King and wanting God's name to be above all names.

This psalm gives so much meaning to the heart transplant we are going through in our lives and our marriages. Turning back to God, asking to be cleansed, for a renewed heart, and a statement seeking prosperity in our marriages. That God will be glorified in the story of repentance and restoration to come.

David's heart is in the right place in this Psalm. Does he get it right every time after he finishes speaking these words? Unfortunately not, but we won't either. We must focus on the best of our heart right now, as we remember (1) our Father's Unfailing Love; (2) plea for God to Cleanse Me and Don't Leave Me; (3) declare that God Use My Broken Spirit; and (4) saying May it Please the Lord in the blessings of life and our marriage to come.

Step V
TRANSFORMED AFTER THE STORM

There are many marriages that will silently make it through a marital storm. Some will deal with things head on and some will shove things under a rug quick to never bring it up again. The difference between a couple that thrives after a storm and a couple that barely survives all depends on the transformation up ahead.

Chapter 10
Mental Storms

The secret to any lasting weight loss transformation happens when more than just our appearances change. The people that reach their goals with the most significant long-term results are the people who went through a mental transformation along the way. They teach their bodies to respond to food differently. Food becomes a source of energy and not just entertainment. Their behaviors change because they have changed the way they think about staying active and the nutrition they put in their bodies.

When we survive a storm in our marriage we want the shifts to turn into a lifestyle of healthy living, which means we need to do more than just look good on the outside, we need to dissect our mind and overcome some of the battles that take place within our brain.

In chapter 7, we talked about the emotions that are seen through the storms in our life, and we learned about the tight connection between the mind and the body, and as our transformation is taking shape, there is some mental work we need to do on our way out of this storm. If only our behaviors change, then it is our behaviors that will prevent us from walking into this storm again, but more needs to happen. As we go through healing for ourselves and in our marriage's we need to go through a full act of repentance, and repentance requires work done within our mind.

Our worldly view of repentance deals with the person completely being over the thing they are asking to be forgiven for. Our human nature deems us to want to forgive someone once they are changed and made new. We need to be mindful not to confuse our human nature with Biblical truth. In Biblical reference, the word "repentance" is a Greek noun, metanoia, which means "a change of mind". Repentance isn't being changed and made new but a step closer in the refinement process. In seeking repentance, we are beginning a work of creating a shift in our minds.

When temptation in our life creeps into the point that we act on it, more is at work than behavior. Sin has a connection with our mind, and it is a mental shift as much as it is a behavioral battle. Acting out in sin is only a factor in the sin equation, the biggest struggle is the mind.

More than Removing Temptation

In any weight loss plan, one of the first steps is to remove the temptation of bad foods from the pantry. You know that stash of Halloween candy that is still in a bag on the top shelf and that gallon of ice cream in the back of the freezer. The stuff around the house that when you are craving something sweet you have access to the goods. By ridding your pantry and fridge of the wrong foods, you remove the temptation to grab them in a moment of weakness. A good strategy for you, but bad news for everyone else in the house that loves those secret stashes. Limiting the food you have access to is helpful in your weight loss plan, but the reality is that if you don't change your brain and the way your mind looks at those foods you won't see many long-term benefits.

Access is everywhere, even outside your house. Any time I try to eat healthier, my kids seem to be swarmed with birthday party invitations. I admit I have a cake weakness. Not just to eat it, I love to critique the frosting and the density of the cake, it's an activity my husband and I do together. For Matt and I, going to a kids' birthday party is a mini version of us able to be judges on Cupcake Wars.

Removing temptation from my house doesn't remove temptation in its entirety. If we don't tackle temptations pull on us, roots in our mind of this sin storm will linger and control us. The way you think about something will determine how you respond to it. When you think differently, you do differently.

What I want you to know is that removing opportunity is only a part of recovering from sin, the real work comes with cleansing your mind from this weakness. Cleansing our mind is where proactive strength for living an abundant life moving forward comes from.

Often our quick response is that with time everything will be right again. If we can just remove the temptation of sin from someone's life, everything will go back to normal, and we can live a peaceful life once more. Moving to a remote island where all aspects of temptation from alcohol, drugs, internet use, or other males or females should do the trick, but it doesn't. The removal of temptation may be helpful at the initial stages, but it is hard to make any full recovery if our healing is limited to "don't do it again", "don't be around it". More is at stake in the process of overcoming, finding freedom, and feeling healed.

Jesus threw the world for a loop when he said to the crowd "You have heard that it was said, 'You shall not commit adultery.' But I tell you that anyone who looks at a woman lustfully has already committed adultery with her in his heart" (Matthew 5:27,28). The heart doctor is seen examining the intricacy of the condition and purity of our mind concerning sin. Our world tends to focus more on the seen over the unseen, but not Jesus, He knows that the heart, mind, and our behaviors are all connected. They all make up us as a person and influence the decisions we make or fight not to make. The pursuit to holiness is a calling on our life, but one that requires more than just living a life that looks like Jesus. Conforming to the image of Christ means to develop the character of Christ. To be one with Him in mind, body, and spirit. What a challenge!

In Matthew 5, Jesus goes further into this description to display the power of removing the things that lead us to sin. "If your right eye causes you to sin, gouge it out and throw it away (5:29)". I am not sure just how literal he meant this, but when Jesus speaks you listen intently. His words are with a passion to the extent that you can feel that he understood the real struggle of sin in our lives. There are times when we admit defeat and learn that a specific temptation has more control over us than we have over it, and that's when its removal becomes imperative, at least for a time while you regain strength from the power God gives you. Other than that, the root of sin is a battle in the mind that you will take with you no matter how far away that deserted island is.

This is the reason I believe the bible doesn't instruct only to repent and turn away – even if that's all you hear your friends telling you right now. We are told to "repent, then, and turn to God" (Acts 3:19) because we need to turn to God to be able to cleanse our mind from sin. It is only after we accept and admit our sin and work through the cleansing of our mind that we can work on becoming cleansed from it. Repenting becomes more of a process than a deliberate step of action.

Rehab

I remember hearing a couple give their story after the husband battled a severe alcohol addiction, the wife told me the story of hope she had in watching her husband go to rehab. She was convinced that rehab was the answer to her husband's addiction. She believed that once rehab was over he would come back home and they would have the normal life she had wanted without this addiction being present again.

She attended her first Al-Anon meeting and was crushed to hear another woman talking about this being her husband's third time at Rehab.

"What…" she thought to herself, "how many times is this going to take?".

She realized in that meeting that this was a bigger struggle than just the removal of behavioral patterns. The person struggling with the addiction has to want it, to choose it, and cleanse their mind to a place where they begin to one day at a time make decisions in line with their new lifestyle.

When I spoke to this woman's husband, he gave me his testimony as he looks back at going through this over 30-years ago and still remembers the location of the alcohol section at their local grocery store at the time. He remembers having to go to the store to get milk after rehab, that he had to consciously walk the longer route around the store so that he could avoid even walking past the alcohol that once controlled him.

This is what the cleansing of the mind looks like. Behavior and opportunity are a part of recovery, but there is more to be tackled if we are searching for healing and wanting freedom. We have to make an inward transformation in our mind as well as an outward transformation in our actions.

Agreements

The other work in making a shift in your mind from sins sneaky deceit is to separate the true and false statements that linger in your mind. When we sin, we tend to make some false mental agreements that actually helped us justify that our sin was "ok". We make a false agreement when we tell ourselves that our marriage is in turmoil so it's "ok" that I am gossiping and slandering my husband's name to all of our family and friends. Or we make the agreement that it's "ok" to be with other women because my wife hasn't given me attention in years. Or we make the agreement that "I deserve this in my life". Or another false agreement is someone recovering from an addiction saying it's "ok" as long as it's on the weekend. Spouses with a pornography addiction make the agreement in their mind that it is "ok" because "It's not hurting anyone".

There are all kinds of agreements we make, and recognizing the sin we committed is only one step, the other is recognizing the false agreements we made that put us in a fog of being sensitive to our sinful actions. Keep your journal ready or that notes section on your smartphone handy to jot down anytime you notice something pop-up that I am calling agreement triggers. These are the triggers that are connected with your past sin that will immediately take you back to a place in your life when you made a false agreement. Agreement triggers are people, places, or things that are now connected with that season or sin in your life. It is that place you pass that reminds you of those moments you wish to forget, or a song that is now associated with that season of your life, or a website or ad that used to be the door that invited you into your current regrets.

The reason we have to be aware of them is that they are the new battle of the mind. You are choosing a new way to make decisions, which means it will take some time to teach your body a new way to endure those triggers. They are mental traps that want to take you back, and you will need to remember every time an agreement trigger presents itself the new truths and reality that you are clinging to in your life.

Every statement about your sin, the thoughts from the people around you, and especially the thoughts of your spouse need to be filtered in your mind before you believe everything your mind clings to. Just because you think it, doesn't mean it's true. There are going to be moments where you are going to have to tell your brain the sky is blue when it is arguing with you that it is a shade of green, but you are going to have to just accept the truth and not believe everything your brain has been telling you.

The battle of the mind is imperative as we have to combat and redirect the connection between our minds and our hearts. If we are to give our spouses our whole hearts, we need to give them our full minds as well.

/ / Exercise: Mind Games / /

What are some of the agreements you have made either on your path into sin or that you are making about yourself or your spouse as you both go through this recovery? This is where you need to have real honesty with yourself and begin to combat the agreements you made during a sensitive place in your life and the truths that you know about your life. Another aspect I am adding to this exercise is an element of God's promises. It may take you some time to be able to fill in that last column so if you need to leave it blank for now don't fret about it, but my prayer is that you come back to it. The promises are what you know God says about the false belief you are struggling with in your life.

	Observation	False Belief	What's Real	God's Truth
Example:	Matt doesn't tell me he loves me enough.	I am not loved.	Matt does love me, I just don't see it at times.	*"I have loved you with an everlasting love."* Jeremiah 31:3
1.				
2.				
3.				
4.				
5.				
6.				
7.				
8.				
9.				
10.				

Chapter 11
Choosing Forgiveness

If you looked at the table of contents, some of you have jumped to this chapter. You are in a position where you need to forgive someone who has hurt you. The hurts and betrayals that you have experienced have victimized your heart, and you are unsure how you will ever find peace with that person again. In a flash, before your eyes, everything has changed, everything is different. The person you once knew seems gone. You don't want to forgive because you want them to experience your level of disappointment and pain. That's why it's essential you read up until this part of the book because getting to a place of acceptance is the first path you have to go down.

The path of accepting your current circumstances is a hard reality to face, but necessary to reach and receive repentance in your life. Whether you have hope that your marriage is going to work out or not, acceptance and repentance allow healing to take place over the hurt in the relationship. Even if you both end up walking away from each other after all this, my prayer is that you still find a way to seek and ask for forgiveness from one another. Forgiveness is a part of marriage, but it is also bigger than marriage, it should exist both inside and outside of it. So for now, let's put aside the lingering doubts of "Are we going to make it?", and understand that whether you make it or not, we should all practice having a heart towards forgiveness in our lives.

Now is not the time for making a clear-cut decision for your marriage. Emotionally your world has been shattered, and nothing in life makes sense. Making a major decision for your marriage, yourself, or even your environment can be a decision you will regret. Before you make any major moves in your life, get to a place where you can slightly breathe again. Be careful of making reactionary decisions for your life when you haven't even considered forgiveness yet. Without a heart shift, the choices we make in a reactionary moment will be decisions that will ease the feelings we have at that moment, which aren't always best for ourselves or our marriages long-term. In a state of panic and without a notion of forgiveness we can quickly make short-term decisions that will make things easier right now but won't provide the true healing you will need for long-term recovery.

Giving forgiveness during difficult times in your life will teach you more about the character of Christ than you could learn through any other avenue. You cannot go entirely through the process of forgiving without a deeper understanding of being forgiven. This level of knowledge you are about to gain is rare, and this is what I meant at the beginning about the growth spurt underway in your life. Forgiveness is a character trait that will grow you at an emotional and spiritual level that most people won't understand if they haven't had to go through this level of extreme forgiveness.

Forgiveness is not popular; forgiveness isn't that pretty either. But forgiveness is powerful. And forgiveness will work at your soul to produce something so beautiful in your life because it will change the way you see everything out your window. It will change the way you even see yourself.

Forgiveness will tear down the walls of entitlement. Forgiveness will cut through the surface of pride. Forgiveness will shine the light of love on the areas in your relationship you've spotlighted with hate.

Forgiveness will play a part in changing the world because it changed it when Christ first gave it. Forgiveness influences everything because it becomes an expression of how we love. It's hard, and it's messy. And asking someone to forgive you is both humbling and humiliating.

But it is freedom. This chapter is about forgiveness, and it's about freedom. Forgiveness will bring freedom. For you both. It will bring surrender. And it will insert love in every crevice that division wants to rule. Forgiveness will provide strength over the false sense of security that un-forgiveness tries to provide.

There is power and freedom in forgiveness. Let's talk about how to do that.

Compassion

When brokenness and compassion collide in the same moment, love becomes magnified. Compassion will change you. Compassion will challenge you. Compassion will teach you empathy in the areas of your life you are blinded to. Both compassion and forgiveness are two of the secrets to leading a Christ-centered and love-filled marriage, they are essential in every marriage no matter what happens, big or small. It's in the moments of your marriage when brokenness is highlighted, and compassion intercedes, that unconditional love is displayed.

How we handle seeing our spouses brokenness will influence how we love. Dr. Cloud and Dr. Townsend describe how to manage the reality of being married to an imperfect being in Boundaries in Marriage:

> "So, the question becomes, "What then?" What do you do when your spouse fails you in some way or is less than you wish for him to be? What happens when she has a weakness or a failure? How about an inability to do something? What about an unresolved childhood hurt that he brings to the relationship?
>
> Other than denial, there are only a couple of options. You can beat your spouse up for their imperfections, or you can love them out of them. The Bible says, "Love covers over a multitude of

sins" (1 Peter 4:8). Nothing in a relationship has to destroy that relationship if forgiveness is in the picture. No failure is larger than grace. No hurt exists that love cannot heal. But for all of these miracles to take place, there must be compassion and forgiveness." (Cloud, 1999, p. 136-137).

God didn't love us because we first loved Him, but the other way around and we have to learn that we forgive because we are also forgiven and loved unconditionally. Loved unconditionally and forgiven unconditionally. God has shown us a level of compassion beyond our wildest imaginations. There is power in that statement above declaring that "no failure is larger than grace", do you feel the power in those words? Just wow! Forgiveness isn't just something we do to get over conflict and head to a fast track towards peace. Forgiveness is a lesson in love. It teaches us to believe the words we read in scripture that "love covers a multitude of sins". When we struggle with forgiveness, we struggle with love.

When someone you love dearly is on the path of healing and recovery from a dark period in their life, there are still attacks keeping them stuck in the state of feeling unworthy, unlovable, and tossed aside. They have hurt you, and the hardest thing you will hear me say is that they had a choice, and it seems like we are all here in this spot because they made the wrong one. What you may be too emotional to realize at this point is that you now have a choice as well. They made the wrong choice in succumbing to the temptation of sin, but how you handle the sin is now your decision to make.

When you stand before one another in acknowledgment that you are both sinners, know that the position you both sit in could easily be reversed and there could be a time in your marriage where you are asking for the forgiveness that is being asked of you to give right now. Placing yourself in a leveled position with your spouse at this moment, or anyone you need to forgive will help the heart shift towards forgiveness. We can too quickly forget that "we have an unholy propensity for desiring mercy when we have harmed others but being stingy in offering it to those that have harmed us" (Kuligan, 2006, p. 166). Said another way, when we harm others we are eager for their forgiveness of us but can be reluctant in our ability to give it when we have been harmed by someone else.

Sin and the Sinner

The best way to begin the process of forgiveness for someone you care about, or anyone in the world for that matter, is to separate the sin and the sinner. Without this necessary step, it's hard to see a heart behind your hurt. Here's what I mean, over and over I see the tendency to dehumanize a person after we see sin. It's hard to see a spouse after sin. It's hard to see a best friend after sin. It's hard to see a person after sin. It's hard even to see an American citizen once they receive the guilty verdict. After sin surfaces, it's hard to look into the eyes of our spouse and see anything but sin at that moment. When sin and the sinner are the same, we almost remove the soul of the person standing before us. I struggled with this in my marriage.

When I found out about the storm my husband brought into our marriage, I didn't know how I would ever look at him the same again. I was so angry. What my flesh wanted to do was give in to the instinct to hurt him back and make him sorry for what he had done to me. In my loneliest moments of shock and anger, Matt didn't even feel like a human to me anymore. It was like someone just walked in and told me that the husband I knew was dead and I was grieving the loss of him as if he wasn't still in the house with me anymore. I was depressed, insecure, and left feeling unloved. I had trouble even looking at him. In my eyes, he was no longer a sinner; he was just sin.

I cannot stress enough the bondage you will feel in your own life without forgiveness. Forgiveness is not just for them it's also for you. For both of you. I share my honesty in hopes that you can be intentional about your choices in moments where my husband and I made decisions based solely on our instincts. I needed to forgive him, fully forgive him. And I needed to separate the sin from the sinner. But I didn't. I told myself "he doesn't love me", and "he never really cared about me", and that "he isn't the best thing for me", and I made decisions I can't take back because I believed those lies.

I gave myself false permission to sin justifying that I needed to understand his sin to forgive him. Please, please, I am begging you, this is not a road you want to go down. I write that because I believe your instincts may be in a similar place. I am giving you pieces of my testimony, but I have also heard the same story unfold from couples in crisis in my counseling office. Sin happens when we are most vulnerable and sensitive to it, and right now, the emotional and most vulnerable person is you, the one who feels deeply hurt by the situation you are both in. You have been mistreated, left to feel like you don't matter and weren't important, but if you aren't careful, the sin cycle is about to start with you. The beliefs and statements you make right now will play a significant role in how you feel about the other person and the decisions you make next.

There is no permission that any of us are given to sin. We make choices. Without separating the sin from the sinner, you run a huge, volatile risk of making the next person who needs to ask forgiveness be you.

Can he/she still love me if they hurt me?

Our immediate response when a loved one has brought sin into our lives is that they don't love us. How is it even possible to love someone you have hurt? My entire life I have struggled hearing people tell me how much my Dad loved my sister and me, but I didn't believe them. It always felt like words with no meaning. "It can't be possible to love your kids so much and commit suicide never to get to experience life with them", that was my thinking. I chose to spend most of my adolescent life believing the agreement in my mind that he must not have loved me as much as everyone said he did. I would stare at the picture of the toddler version of myself on his lap with smiles on both of our faces and think that it must not have been real. He must not have loved me to have hurt me in this way. Flash forward to being an adult, and I was faced with the same question, now towards my husband, "Can he love me and hurt me like this?". The circumstances were different, but the feelings were strangely the same.

I am learning today what my heart couldn't comprehend before now; sin doesn't make sense. There is no logic behind it, and we are all susceptible to it. Sin is destruction. Sin always says "one more time", it still wants more, it wants to stay close, and it wants to remain hidden.

Without the hope of forgiveness, we can turn sin into a blame game that will turn into a lifestyle of blaming. But when you play the sin blame game where do you end? Each sin has an emotional attachment to an unmet longing or desire in someone's life. If I blame my husband, should I also blame all the other factors that led to his susceptibility? Do I blame my Dad for bailing on me, and then blame the circumstances to his depression and the actions he took?

There is no end to where the blame trail will lead you, so don't make that your objective. As a Jesus follower, and with our fallen nature, if temptation and sin grab hold of our heart, we must know that love hasn't let go of it. We don't give in to sin because we are void of love but because we misuse and abuse its existence.

When we ask ourselves the question of "how can they say they love me after what they did to me?" remind yourself of the damage and twists of sin. As we get through the storm, we need to believe we are loved, even when we struggle to feel it. We have to work to believe we're loved, even if we don't understand it, with the hope that reassurance and the feelings to match it will come.

Worthy of Forgiveness

The biggest blessing we can give each other through forgiveness is saying through words and actions that you are worth forgiving, our marriage is worth forgiving, our family is worth forgiving, and that you are worth fighting for. When we practice forgiveness, we practice love, and any time we practice love we show someone they have worth.

How you have been taught forgiveness will shape how you give it, or if you give it at all. If three strikes and you're out is the way you have been taught forgiveness you might need to rethink your definition. When your definition is skewed, it interrupts your ability to show forgiveness. You may have been taught that forgiveness is earned, and you may have been taught that you are naïve if you keep forgiving, but those are upside down versions of the kingdom of God we are bringing here to the earth.

If your heart is beating, you are worthy of forgiveness. Trust may need to be earned, but forgiveness is an unmerited gift. If forgiveness needed to be earned, you and I would both be in for some trouble. God made a plan for a world that needed a plan because we can't earn forgiveness. God knew the options were to let us try to earn it or He could freely give it. The fruit that is birthed out of this storm, the storm we wish never happened in our marriages, will be the alignment of matching our hearts to God. You and your spouse need to recognize the same sin dilemma in your relationship. The options are to let them spend the rest of their lives trying to earn forgiveness or making the decision to give it freely. When we live with a mindset of "deserving" and "earning", we will never be satisfied, we will never find the peace we seek because we are putting our hope into a world that is fleeting and into people that on their best days are still self-seeking.

Instead, we need to see the worth of a person not depending on a hierarchy scale but a leveled platform. The spotlighted sinner in front of you at the dinner table has the same level of worth that you do. Once you understand there is nothing they can do to deserve forgiveness thoroughly, you can give them the gift of worth by extending undeserved forgiveness to them.

Don't Give Up

Without a blend of compassion and forgiveness, we could end up saying, "since we hurt each other, might as well throw in the towel, start over, put this dusty broken marriage on the back shelf of the store with all the other items to be thrown out".

The words of this world will say break away; break ties; this person isn't good for you; you deserve better; there is plenty of fish in the sea; protect yourself; give up, and the sayings go on. From my experience, when the world responds to a storm with division and isolation, more storms will arise on the horizon. "Let's just go our separate ways" doesn't include the character growth that Jesus wants to see come out of this storm. "I am giving up on you because it looks like you have given up on me" cannot be the go-to response when a storm hits in our marriage.

How thankful are we that God never talks to us like that – or even the Israelites in the Old Testament? We would all be lost. As Christians, we are called to be heaven on earth, even with people that haven't treated us like we hope to see in heaven.

Will some marriages end in divorce after major trials have surfaced? Yes, and that may be after several attempts at trying to make it work. What I am emphasizing right now is not making the focus the end result of your marriage, but that you at least try to make it work. Even if it doesn't work, you will both grow through even this process of trying and practicing forgiveness. I would go even a step further and boldly say that this is more about growing in your character and relationship with God than whether your marriage stays together or ends in divorce. Just hear my plea not to give up, and that forgiveness and healing are possible in impossible situations.

Forgiveness is a Choice

However this storm occurred, you may feel as though you have been left choice-less. The intrusion of this storm may or may not have been you're doing, but making an alignment with sin is a choice and a choice that everyone around you is impacted by. Don't underestimate the power of me saying that forgiveness is a choice too. We can't use our sensitivities as excuses for our sins our entire lives, and both spouses also can't use the fact that your loved one sinned as an excuse for your lack of forgiveness either.

If you've already admitted you didn't like the choice your loved one made, now please, with a tender heart, decide what choice you are going to make. You have a choice in what to do with this storm. You get to choose what to fight for, you get to decide to treat someone like they have worth, and you get to choose the responses you are about to give. God can do remarkable things with a repentant heart, don't give up on them or your marriage too quickly. Forgiving is an act of giving something to someone else; it is a choice and a hard one to make, but necessary on the path of healing and recovery.

Hear me again say that forgiveness is a choice too. If you wait for your "heart to be in the right place" to allow yourself to forgive you may still be married 30-years from now waiting for that forgiving heart to come. It won't come without you choosing it. Choose to forgive, and remember that you are a sinner as well, and may even have things you need to ask forgiveness for in your marriage. You know what, I am not going to say maybe, I bet you do, I bet you have things you need to ask forgiveness for. I promise humility isn't as scary as your pride wants you to believe it is.

Once you choose to forgive, you then need to make decisions and plan responses that are in line with the choice you've made. Your feelings may give you reminders that you haven't forgiven, so you will need to remind yourself of the choice you've made. You will have days where it is easy and days where your "heart just isn't in the right place", on both of those days, remind yourself that you are choosing to forgive.

Barriers to Forgiveness

<u>Barrier #1: "My heart just isn't in the right place".</u>

Over and over I have heard the Christian response from people, "my heart just isn't in the right place to forgive right now". I am going to try to write this out as soft as possible even though there is a passion my voice wants to give when I hear that statement.

So here's the thing, I praise Jesus that on the day of the cross he didn't look to the Father and say, "my heart just isn't in the right place to do this today". Do you know how we get stretched, how we grow, and how we learn to love and live a life that goes beyond our human nature? I'll tell you; we do things that are against the fleshly nature of our heart for the sake of being obedient and in line with our Father. It is not until after we have done the uncomfortable, the unnatural, and the un-instinctual that we look back and say, "Oh, I see what you just did there God".

We don't live that way, do we? We want to understand. We want to know how the whole story will unfold before we accept the script to play a role we are unfamiliar with. Giving forgiveness is that unfamiliar role. We don't know how to give forgiveness or extend a heart of grace to people unless we understand the other person and our reasoning for forgiveness fully. We need a case pleaded for us that gives us beyond a shadow of a doubt results that point us to forgiveness. We need to be talked into it.

When you wait for your heart to be in the right place, you will be waiting a long time, and you also don't live with the real understanding that your heart is full of sins tugs just as much as the sinner before you. We all need to lower our stature for just a moment to recognize that your heart won't just wake up one morning and be in the right place.

Until you realize that your heart is made of flesh, it is just impossible. Without the power of the Holy Spirit, you won't be able to get there, because your human nature will point you away from doing the very things that are against your heart to begin with. We need to turn the saying "waiting for my heart to be in the right place" into the new saying of "making decisions because they are in the right place with the heart of the Father".

Just as Jesus gained the attention of many for his counter-culture reaction to sinners, so are we called to have a counter heart in the way we live our lives. We can't live our lives doing whatever place our heart happens to be on that day. The desires of the flesh will lead us straight to sin, and this is why you are sitting here even having to forgive your spouse for something to begin with, because they followed in line with the position of their heart instead of turning to and aligning with a heart of Jesus in the decisions they made.

Now it's your turn. Now you have to do the counterculture act of doing what is against your heart, and aligning with matching that of Christ. This is how we become one with Him, to share a heart, to share a response, and to live a life with an extreme amount of love that gets the heads turning of everyone around you. By making one obedient decision at a time that is against your heart and in line with God's.

We don't want to forgive just because we've got all the facts and details now; or because enough "time" has gone by so now you're ready; or because it all makes sense now why it all happened in the first place; or because you witness the person has been made new. Trust desires because statements, but forgiveness warrants faith. Forgiveness comes without a because; forgiveness grows us when we give it while it doesn't make sense yet at all. Your heart won't be in the right place to forgive, so don't wait for that day to come. Waiting for your heart to change is just one of the barriers to forgiveness.

Barrier #2: It's Personal

Another barrier to forgive is taking sin at a personal level. It is hard to forgive when we look at sin as an intentional attack. These are one of those agreements you need to avoid that I mentioned earlier.

137

If you believe at your core that the person that hurt you has a good heart, then don't agree with seeing them as a vindictive monster that had a plot out for your demise. That agreement and negative voice will become a poison that will prevent healing and moving forward. When you make that agreement in your heart, you will spend most of your life waiting for their next attack because deep down they are still the monster you shaped them to be in your head.

When someone else's sin feels personal to you, the hurt and pain you are dealing with will also seem intentional. It will look like they did this on purpose to hurt you. In an emotional state, this will be a struggle you go through. Taking their sin as a personal attack at you could be the enemy's attempt at grabbing your heart to keep you from ever finding peace. "They wanted to hurt you. They are smiling at your demise. They are enjoying the suffering and pain you have to go through right now." Why? "Because you deserve it, you deserve all this misery", that's at least what you believe they think when you take it personally.

When my husband and I were able to look at each other as struggling sinners instead of war rivals out to get each other, that is when our forgiving hearts could start to take shape. Once we saw each other as a sinner and not the embodiment of sin, our hearts changed FOR one another instead of AGAINST one another.

Barrier #3: Aggressive Instinct

When we believe our spouse is against us, it will be hard to see anything other than aggression, and when we are driven by aggression, it will put up a wall making it that much harder to forgive. Our aggression could be one of our most significant barriers to forgive.

We can understand aggression a little more by learning about our aggressive instinct, and what kind of counselor would I be if I didn't educate you guys a bit. You're in for a treat, because who better to help us with this than Alfred Adler, who is known as the father of Individual Psychology. Adler introduced the concept of an individual approach to treating people on their unique nature but in developing this theoretical practice he went through an educational learning curve of different understandings in the field of psychology. He spent a lot of time in the earlier 1900's studying and writing on the concept of 'drive psychology' and in particular coined an 'aggressive drive'. His way of thinking later shifted in moving from a stance of aggression as an innate drive, to believing it involves an element of a natural desire to overcome.

In his recounting of his initial discovery, he writes: "In 1908 I hit upon the idea that every individual really exists in a state of permanent aggression, and I was imprudent enough to call this attitude the 'aggression drive'. But I soon realized that I was not dealing with a drive, but with a partly conscious, partly irrational attitude towards the tasks which life imposes; and I gradually arrived at an understanding of the social element in personality, the extent of which is always determined by the individual's opinion of the facts and difficulties of life" (Adler, 1956, p. 38). Adler goes further into pointing us on the path of understanding that "every unsatisfied drive ultimately orients the organism toward aggression against the environment. The rough characters and the unbridled, incorrigible children can instruct us in the way the continuously unsatisfied drive for affection stimulates the paths of aggression" (Adler, 1956, p. 42).

Besides the fact that we see Adler refer to us as mere "organisms" in his description lies a lot of secular but real truth to the formation of our bodies. On your path to forgiving, aggression is the barrier that will keep you stuck. We get stuck because our aggression has more to do with our unsatisfied drives and our opinions of our circumstances more than the circumstance itself. Learning what the aggression is trying to overcome can help you deal with the root barrier. Your extended aggression could have more to do with things outside your current circumstance than you realize. There could be a wound attached to you that you are overcoming with the ongoing aggression you are directing at your spouse.

Adler described our way of dealing with some of our root issues by subconsciously "transforming our drives into its opposite" (Adler, 1956, p. 32). An example can be our current desire for affection towards our spouse, but instead, we transform that feeling into its opposite, aggression. You never thought you would be an adult still waking up to play the opposite game, did you? Funny how our childhood games can stem from our unconscious mind, and even crazier to think that some of the most aggressive couples are secretly longing for affection and connectedness with their spouse.

As you practice the discipline of forgiveness, notice within yourself the hardships and voids that will get in the way of being able to see the brokenness in your spouse at this moment. One of the best ways to move from aggression to compassion is to look at yourself and see elements of brokenness that you have as well.

God's Grace helps our Forgiveness

The book, Ten Things I Wish Jesus Never Said, by Victor Kuligan, goes through ten important things that Jesus said that are hard truths for Christians to hear but pivotal in not being overlooked as we try to emulate Christ's character to the best of our ability. He goes on quite passionately in the chapter on the Art of Forgiveness quoting Jesus' statement that "If you do not forgive others their sins, your Father will not forgive your sins" (Matt 6:15; Mark 11:26). Pretty powerful words said by Jesus that sometimes our pen meant to underline in our Bibles scribbles right over that line with how daunting that task is to our lives.

Forgiveness is a discipline in character formation, one that we cannot deny no matter the marital storm you are in, which includes any friends and family involved as well. Our spiritual formation will take shape as we learn how forgiving others helps us understand the unmerited grace that God has shown upon us. Kuligan puts it in this form: "we will always have a tendency to harbor bitterness and grudges as long as we misunderstand God's mercy shown to us." It is more important in our spiritual walk with God to get to a place where we recognize that all God has given us is completely undeserved, and only through that heart identification can we fully realize that if "I receive all I have as if I am a beggar, then granting others forgiveness becomes easy. Yes, I said easy, not easier. When we recognize that our entire relationship with God is undeserved grace – favor shown to us when all we deserve is punishment and God's wrath – granting forgiveness to others should be easy for us" (Kuligan, 2006, p. 166).

We can't talk about forgiveness without realizing that we are also forgiven. We have to start there, we have to end there, and really, we shouldn't ever leave there, or we'll forget it. You have been forgiven. That thing that's hard for you to do right now (give forgiveness), it's been given to you. That thing you're struggling to ask for forgiveness from, or that secret you still haven't shared with your spouse – your God forgives you. You have been forgiven. Forgiven people, forgive people.

Broken Together

So here's the thing, I have never met a blameless spouse. I have never sat down with a couple without uncovering that they both have a reason to ask for forgiveness. We could argue which person's struggle is uglier than the other, but that is beyond the point I am making here at this moment. I have never met a blameless spouse. You will find the most beauty when you sit broken together and not perfect and pointing a finger.

One of the most humbling places you may find yourself in marriage is getting the opportunity to sit broken together. I know it's crazy that I said "opportunity", but I say that because no matter what we go through, we have to deal with the reality that we married a sinner that has struggles and sensitivities to sins tempting attacks on their life. We all have weakness within us, and we will all have seasons where the weaknesses we struggle with may even be the ones we never knew we had. We shouldn't welcome sin, but we should expect temptation.

We all have struggles, and the fault in my marriage was probably not talking about these as proactively as we should have from the start. We believed the best to an unrealistic level not expecting storms to ever be a hurdle in our lives. We believed our love was enough to get us through anything and fight any battle, but it's God's love and our obedience to Him that will get us through any situation. Our sin is great, and thankfully, God's love is greater. Being broken together allows couples to heal together and then also allows them to connect together beautifully. Not as one person superior to the other but as we both reconnect with the message of redemption and the Gospel.

Even on the darkest days of our marriage, the beautiful pictures on the wall of our wedding and our family are still beautiful; they are just pictures of two sinners in love learning what it means to love one another completely. My kids are still all young, but as they grow, the new lesson my husband and I will have to learn is what to do with the fact that our children aren't the saints we thought we raised either. They will have sin storms that blow through their lives and watching us humbly be broken with them will grow them more than only condemning their hearts.

Journal: Matt and I have spent the past four months doing nothing but reading, praying, listening to music, and talking to each other. Everything in our lives right now is about turning back to our Father and repositioning where we are before Him. We have so many voices in our life right now telling us what to say, how to respond, and what to do next but not everyone is giving us advice that is matching how we see God's response to this storm. We are having to turn to God as intimately as we can so that His voice can be louder than the rest.

You can learn the path of restoration when you choose to forgive each other while recognizing you are broken together. For some people, it takes longer to get to this point, but from the couples I have helped, the stories I have heard, and the personal experience I have walked in, repairing your marriage gains the most healing once you both realize that two sinners got married to each other. Lowering your stature next to your spouse as an equal in the struggle to overcome sin makes it easier to forgive than making yourself superior and self-righteous in believing they are alone as the only sinner in the relationship. Again, I have never met a blameless spouse.

Forgiveness is a topic I could talk about at length with you. Practicing forgiveness shouldn't be done only if the marriage stays together. You will find healing to the hardest hurts in your life in learning to forgive whether you end up still married to your partner or divorced. Even though forgiveness is a controversial topic and rarely practiced today, in my experience, it is completely transformational. If this chapter on forgiveness is the only thing you apply from this book, I believe a transformation will take place in you. You cannot practice forgiveness without it changing who you are as a person. Forgiveness is a lesson in love. How Jesus teaches us to understand forgiveness, and the discipline it requires, will put you another step closer to finding peace and joy through the storm.

Chapter 12
Freedom

If every sin has a story, then every restoration has a story too. You will find comfort hearing the stories of friends and mentors that have gone through dark storms in their lives and made it out to breathe the fresh air on the other side. You have probably already found yourself researching stories online to search for evidence of hope after all this. Your desire is freedom. Can I feel free after all of this?

There is evidence of God's handiwork among the mess our hands have created, but we have to remember that as we look at the stories of others, our recovery story will be its own story. We are on a path to Freedom, but know that our timeline for healing will look different than others. When we do the middle right and focus on the full aspect of repent, turn towards God, and become transformed, the end can look the same...transformed. The end can be filled with a peace that truly does surpass all understanding, and a walk into Freedom you couldn't have even fathomed before all of this. Let's dig through the residue left behind from this storm to find Freedom at the other end, and let's pack this chapter with scripture because I can't think of any other way to feel Free.

Value even in the Dirt

Whatever your marriage looks like right now, whatever you look like right now, you have value even among the dirt in your life.

Joyce Meyer gives a great illustration of this as she recalls listening to a speaker that held up a $50 bill to an audience of 200 and asks for hands to raise for anyone that would like that $50. As all the hands are up in the room, the speaker begins to crumple up the bill, write on it, and even step on it a few times and then repeats the same question. Does the fact that the crisp $50 bill looks different and even distorted change the reaction in the room? No. Everyone still has their hands in the air. This is because, despite the appearance of the bill, its value has not changed one bit. (Meyer, 2005, p. 13)

There are people in your life that may look at you right now like your value has changed, they may make you even question your worth. Finding joy and regaining life from all this needs to come from the faith we have in who God says we are, and how He looks at us. God looks at us like our value hasn't changed, and the worth He sees in us is greater than we saw in ourselves before all of this. He knew the extent of our dirt before all of this and created us anyway. While there are people, who don't and maybe never will see what God sees, know that your value hasn't changed. Or perhaps even use this experience as a way to learn that you have value if this is your first time receiving that message; you may never have learned that about yourself before all this.

God doesn't see our value changed because He knows full well what it cost, He was there when He paid it. Amen!

Loved in the Act

Let's look at the well-known story of the adulteress woman a little deeper. And now that you are both going through this crisis in your marriage, you may even notice a widening perspective change on the Biblical stories that seem most familiar. These stories will come to life like they hadn't before. John 8 tells us the story of a woman caught in the act of adultery. We don't hear what happens to the male she was with, but we see the Pharisees realizing this as an excellent opportunity to put Jesus in a corner to see if He follows the laws by which they firmly stood by. After asking Jesus if they should follow the law and stone her, He responds in this way:

"But Jesus bent down and started to write on
the ground with his finger. When they kept on
questioning him, he straightened up and said to
them, "Let any one of you who is without sin be
the first to throw a stone at her." Again, he stooped
down and wrote on the ground." (John 8:6b-8)

We see Jesus in this encounter not quick to respond. We don't
see him jump up and gasp at the drama of this woman brought
to him. He stays bent down and writes in the dust on the ground,
unknown to us what he is writing. Some scholars say the purpose
for not letting us know what he was writing was because he wasn't
writing anything meaningful. The lawmakers were making such a
big ordeal about this woman's sin that Jesus is seen just doodling on
the ground. Much like you do during an uninteresting sermon where
you look down and doodle on the Sunday morning newsletter they
gave you. We see Jesus not even stand up to answer them until they
become persistent at asking him what to do.

Did you notice the patience He has in giving them an answer?
How often do we hear of someone's sin and stand up in quick
reaction with what we are going to do about it? We jump before we
breathe before we calm down and take everything into perspective.
Our human nature puts us in a position when we go through crisis
mode that we lose sight of Christ mode.

Jesus here shows us another response. He stands up and doesn't
tell them not to stone her. Did you catch that? He doesn't say she is
undeserving of punishment, leave her alone. He still knows she is a
sinner, that she is not perfect. Jesus wants everyone around her to
humble themselves before they humiliate her. "Let the first person
without sin throw a stone at her." Can you imagine everyone in the
circle with a stone already in their hands, not a pebble mind you, a
stone ready to throw it? Everyone looking around to see what they
should do. We know that in that circle Jesus would be the only
one qualified to throw a stone at this point, but what does he do,

the scripture says "he stoops down and wrote on the ground". It seems He would rather finish his doodle than make a huge deal of humiliating and condemning someone in their sin.

What happens next stuns everyone except Jesus. A woman, with her eyes, probably shut in fear of the pain headed her way and shaking uncontrollably from the situation. Probably clothed with only a blanket wrapped around her because she was caught in the "act" of adultery, so I'm sure they didn't give her the decency of putting clothes on before they publicly shunned her. She hears Jesus' voice and the statement he made to them and then peers her eyes open to watch this next part unfold:

> "At this, those who heard began to go away one at a time, the older ones first, until only Jesus was left, with the woman still standing there. Jesus straightened up and asked her, "Woman, where are they? Has no one condemned you?" "No one, sir," she said. "Then neither do I condemn you," Jesus declared. "Go now and leave your life of sin." (John 8: 10,11)

Wow, just wow! The Pharisees tried to trap Jesus in a corner, but it's just like Jesus to show up again shocking the crowd with his counterculture responses of love. This is a glimpse of undeserved Freedom.

I have heard this story so many times, and every time I do, I hear it from the position of pity. That poor woman being humiliated like that, publicly criticized for a closed-door sin in her life. We don't know her story. We don't know how she got there. We only know the sin and the punishment. There is healing to bringing sin to the light, but not like this.

The broadening perspective we need to gain in our marriages is to find ourselves in a place where you resonate with the characters in this story. Don't look down on it, look at it like you are in it. Are you the sinner in the center of the circle or someone on the outskirts of the crowd ready to throw a stone? Imagine being a stone thrower, not just grabbing any rock off the ground. They are walking around with hardened hearts seeking the stone that will hurt. Much like we look for the perfect skipping rock to throw in a lake, they actively seek out "Oh, this will be a good stone to throw". Imagine the sinner in the center regretting the decisions she's made with no option of turning around, with no way out, in the pit of sin with nothing but death in her future.

Are you feeling it? Are you sitting in this story now? Not hearing it like you have many times before, but sitting in it like it is happening in your family room. Which person are you? Either way, whichever position you find yourself sitting in right now I want you to see the way out. No one sees it; no one sees another path in this story. There is no second option besides stone her for the lawmakers, and the woman sees no other way out but death. Neither of these options sounds like they lead to Freedom.

Up to this point, as we have been dealing with the sin that has entered your marriage, we have had to deal at some level with this scenario. It's time now, time for you to start to see the way out, time to open the door and begin to walk again. We have either witnessed or had to give a confession where the truth has come out, but you don't feel that "the truth will set you free" (John 8:32). This is difficult for each of you. And if you are familiar with that verse from John, it's usually taken out of context. That verse isn't saying that you telling the truth is what is going to set you free, it's understanding God's truth that sets us free. Confessions can be helpful, but don't make confessions your savior. A confession can happen on the path to freedom, but freedom comes from God's truth, not you telling yours.

In a counseling room, when we witness one spouse give a confession, we hear one spouse say, "I feel so much better like a weight has been lifted off my chest that I have been carrying around." That may be great for them, but the other spouse felt free yesterday when they didn't know this was going on. Sometimes the truth sets one person free, and the other spouse now has to begin their journey into freedom from the pain they now feel. One spouse's burden lifted is the other spouse's future weights. They both need to be lifted for your marriage to feel freedom.

What you both need to feel is Jesus in the confrontation. While you may all be in an uproar figuring out a quick, instinctual reaction with how to deal with the acknowledgment of sin, here is the story of Jesus in John 8 stooping down to the ground writing in the dust just taking a breath before finally responding. (If only our churches could pause for a moment and learn how to love.) He then doesn't speak on her behalf but puts everyone on the same playing field. That is leadership. That should be our response to sin.

When you mentally shift this scenario from a woman in the middle and a crowd all around her and into everyone on the same playing field, the outcome of this teaching moment is not just about compassion on the one in the middle. I think when we read this scripture we see it as learning to have compassion on the sinner in the middle, but that's just a snapshot of what's taking place. The reality is that this picture is showing that Jesus doesn't see anyone in the middle because we all are. It's not about compassion for the woman in the middle, it's about Jesus having compassion on them all, on us all. He doesn't just look at the woman and say "go and leave your life of sin" (John 8:11), He says that to them all. As they drop their stones and walk away, He is also displaying to everyone crowded around her to "go and sin no more" as well. This story is not just about her, it's about everyone that showed up that day. That same truth is happening even at your home. As you make your marriage crisis focused on putting one person in the middle of the circle, hear Jesus saying that getting through this storm is about everyone first standing in the middle together.

Before we are quick to judgment, consequence, and justification, we need to clear our heart, and sit down for a minute in the middle of the circle with whoever's sin is being spotlighted in your marriage.

Breathe for a couple of moments, maybe even a few days, and then start thinking about what to do next. In the moment of reaction, we may find ourselves throwing a stone when Jesus is telling you something different. There is a difference between seeing a sinner with a heart and seeing only a heartless sinner.

Which one are you? Is there a stone in your hand? Maybe you have already thrown a couple, and your spouse is still alive, but barely breathing with all the stones that have been thrown at them. Perhaps you haven't thrown one yet, but man are you thinking about it. Sit with your Father and turn this crisis mode into a heart like Christ. Just with humbling yourself so you can come towards them with a Christ-like heart instead of an approaching fist.

Do you see yourself as the sinner in this story? Feeling alone with the loud voices of condemnation and harsh words that cycled around you, or maybe you are hearing them within you? It's time for you to hear Jesus stand up among the crowd. However he does this for you will be unique, but he will stand up and speak to those around you. Jesus won't control what everyone around you does, but he will speak. You aren't alone, and if you have made it to this part of the book and have gone through these steps with us, then you are ready to start believing again in God's truth, or maybe now for the first time, and feel His presence more than just telling yourself He is there. See Him in your living room. He is the voice when you feel like you have no one.

Let's look at some more scriptures to help us on our search for freedom and joy.

Dead Men Tell No Tales

Have you heard the voice of a pirate in your head? The voice that tells you that dead things stay dead. That voice may haunt the sea, but the truth is that no matter the state of your life right now, and no matter the state your marriage is in, we have a God that says that Dead Men wake up and then proclaim the good news! Sorry Captain Jack, you have been mistaken.

As we continue in the desert, we come to where we are at right now, feeling like a pile of dusty dry bones. Our bodies frail and our minds tired of the path we have been on and the unknown of the road up ahead. You need hope at this point, even but a taste to bring energy to your soul. I found it, and I want to share it with you because this moment is when you need to be revived.

Churches do revivals as a form of rejuvenating the soul, of reminding and empowering us of God's good plan in our life and the life of the church. To be revived is to be brought back to life. At this point, that is what we need, and this is what our marriages need. I need to be resuscitated, and new breath put into my lungs.

Have you read Ezekiel lately? An inspiring prophet whose relationship and conversation with the Lord I can only envy. In Ezekiel 37:1-14 God brings him to a valley of dry bones and in verses 4-6 Ezekiel says:

> This is what he says to me, "Prophesy to these bones and say to them, 'Dry bones, hear the word of the Lord! This is what the Sovereign Lord says to these bones: I will make breath enter you, and you will come to life. I will attach tendons to you and make flesh come upon you and cover you with skin; I will put breath in you, and you will come to life. Then you will know that I am the Lord.'"

So here we are, our bodies and our marriages have become now a pile of dry bones that when we have no breath and cold flesh, the world will put a "time of death" stamp on us and declares us dead. God isn't done with your marriage. Sin may have scraped the skin off your body, and God has stripped us to cleanse our soul, and He's not done yet. He says to you the same words that He was prophesying for the people of Israel. In verse 11 we see that the people of Israel are these dry bones, they are saying "Our bones are dried up, and our hope is gone; we are cut off." So, the Lord tells Ezekiel to give them hope, and you need to hear this hope as well. The Lord tells Ezekiel to tell them:

> *Journal: My heart needed to hear the story of Ezekiel and the Dry Bones today. I don't feel it quite yet, but I am empowered by the hope in this story. I long for God to put his Spirit in me so that I may live again and feel the strength in my body I don't have today.*

"This is what the Sovereign Lord says: My people, I am going to open your graves and bring you up from them; I will bring you back to the land of Israel. Then you, my people, will know that I am the Lord when I open your graves and bring you up from them. I will put my Spirit in you, and you will live, and I will settle you in your own land." (Ezekiel 37:12, 13)

He is reviving an army. This is not just the imagery of dry bones becoming average people. He is reviving them and making them strong. Feeling a revival in your life starts by believing that God has the power to do this in your life, that he has the power to breathe into your marriage. He needs to be invited in because He alone has the power to revive. Without the miracle-working God, all we will hear is the flat-lined buzz in the hospital room declaring our death. That flat-lined buzz may even be coming from the voices all around you, from the people that only see the destruction from this storm. It's time now, we have sat in this storm long enough, there is still work that needs to be done, but it's time now to come to life. Start to hear, and believe His voice, God pulling you up from the grave, refashioning your tendons, restoring your skin, and breathing his breath into your lungs as we slowly hear the flat-lined buzz of the monitor begin to beep…beep…beep…as we come back to life. Dead men can tell tales, and your life and your marriage are becoming a story of overcoming and is a tale that will be worth telling.

My sin, Your Glory

So how do we find joy amidst the turmoil of sin that we have created, that we are owning and taking responsibility for? Paul shows us in his letter to Timothy a beautiful example of God's grace:

> "Here is a trustworthy saying that deserves full acceptance: Christ Jesus came into the world to save sinners - of whom, I am the worst. But for that very reason I was shown mercy so that in me, the worst of sinners, Christ Jesus might display his immense patience as an example for those who would believe in him and receive eternal life." (1 Timothy 1:15, 16)

I love when the disciples write with "but" statements. They are throughout scripture, and I believe our lives have hope because of the "but" statements they give us. Paul is not just sitting in his sin at this moment. He is sitting in the fact that he is a sinner. The "but" in this statement is what we are learning to cling to in our lives right now. Living in the freedom of the "but" statements in God's word brings us hope when the destruction of placing our hope in the world fails us.

Jesus wants me to be in heaven with him, can you believe that? He wants that for you too, yes, a sinner like you and I. Our Father made a way and knew that we needed a plan for redemption. Through the most extreme act of humility, Jesus was made low to fulfill a plan so that we could one day be with him. What amazing love! Paul and Timothy both knew what I am learning to glue to my heart, that even when our sin is great, His love for us was and is greater! I had heard that said before and shook my head in agreement with how cool it is that my God loves me more than I can comprehend. It seems the older I get, and with the life experiences I endure, I seem to gain a sense of awareness of what God's love for me means. A year from now I hope to know it even closer. Romans 5:8 reiterates this by stating that Christ died for us to demonstrate God's love for us. You are a part of a grand love story.

The story gets even better. As much as right now the love story is all about a rescue story of US, the beauty is learning what 1 Timothy shows us even more. In this grand outpour of love God uses His plan of redemption to "display his immense patience". Do you know what that means? God uses everything to point back to the glory of Himself. If we believe that to be true in the reality of the birth, death, and resurrection of our Savior while being sinners, can we attempt to believe that He may be able also to use this storm to point the world back to Him as well? To "overcome evil with good" (Romans 12:21) in all this we must sit in humility before our Creator and acknowledge that we are a sinner – all of us, not just the person in the room with their sin highlighted at the moment. We have to sit and wrestle with the acceptance that God can still use a surrendered sinner. Beyond our failings and daily shortcomings is an eloquent Father who continually pursues our heart and puts us back on track. Will you attempt to believe that with me today?

You have Worth

Do you feel the truth in the statements made in this chapter? I know that in my darkest storms, my mind has wondered if God had turned away from me.

I've often asked myself if that is what David felt like through the Psalms, crying out to God while pleading with him not to be silent, feeling the weight of his guilt and the many people that were probably scolding his actions. Maybe your life is looking similar, feeling shame everywhere you go and wondering whether God views you the way you see you right now.

There can be a tendency to personify God; that the way people treat you can feel like a representation of how God is viewing you. When the shame is coming from someone or a group of people who say they are Christians, personifying God can become even more real. You see, when someone states they are a Christian, there is a natural assumption that God agrees with their perspective, and my friends, listen carefully, this is just not true. As Christians, we aim to be like Him, to be one with Him, and to unite in His perspective of the world and the people in it, not the other way around. God doesn't align with us. We aim to come into alignment with Him. We must see people as God does and not believe that God sees people as we do.

The people around you have storms they are walking through, and one of them may have to do with the way they are treating you, even the Christians, they struggle too. Your joy won't come from them, so don't turn to them to find it. Your joy will come as you find truth in your worth, as you find the truth that you are valued, and as you find truth in grace being a real thing and not a figment of your hopeful imagination.

No matter what you are feeling or the statements, you are hearing. You have worth. You can still claim the position of being a child of God, you just happen to be more thankful and understanding of that title than you have ever realized before this moment. You have worth. You have so much worth that you have value and you are qualified to be used by God. God used David, and God is using you too.

Used by God

Working on staff at the local church, I noticed that we did a lot of experimenting on trying to raise volunteers in our ministry areas. No matter the size of the church we always need more volunteers and more leaders. This is not a problem churches have; it's just a part of church life because we all want the same thing, for people to not only attend church but to become a part of the church body, assisting and playing a role in what God is doing there. Often this starts with someone in your life or your small group looking at you and saying: "I see potential in you". (Powerful words to any human being, and a deep longing on the soul of everyone with a heartbeat.) One of the biggest joys of working in ministry is seeing people grow in their spiritual walk and development. To see people scared to death feeling the inadequacy of being a Small Group leader but taking the leap of faith to do it and watch God mold and grow them. Often my leaders were growing more than the people in the groups were, but the group members didn't know it at the time.

Whether you know it or not, you can be used by God. With all the dirt and grime and ugliness you know about your past, even about your yesterday, even about this morning, you can be used by God.

There is a common misperception that only perfect people with a blemish-free life can volunteer and lead a ministry at a church. There is truth to being a person who can live as an example, but blemish free is an unrealistic expectation. If that were the prerequisite to volunteering or leading, we wouldn't have any recruits. Thankfully our God uses people with a messy past and an ugly marriage. He gives us example after example of using a person to build His Kingdom that we wouldn't expect. You know those movies where you don't even have to watch much to guess what is going to happen next, who the bad guy is and who the hero is going to be. You have watched enough movies to know what characters end up doing what, and you could write the script just based on the movie trailer. God shows us plot twists we could never predict.

- When we expect Him to use the older son to be second in command to an entire nation, He uses the youngest.
- When we expect a leader that will be in the lineage of Jesus we don't expect a sinner like David.
- When we expect Him to bring a Savior into the world, we think it's going to be a significant King, but instead, it is a baby of an unmarried couple born in a lowly manger.

The point is that God uses us no matter the life you have

walked and there is so much freedom to be found in being used and fashioned by God. No matter how off course you have gotten you can be redeemed, and your marriage filled with deception, heartache, and sorrow, can be filled with joy and love you may never have known before. You have trapped yourself long enough in the suffering and pain associated with the recovery from sin. It's time now, you've gone through the hurt, now permit yourself to feel Free. You are a son or daughter of Christ. It's time to walk with your head held high. That's the label on your chest, not the tattoo of your sin. You have worth. You belong to God, now live your life with the joy and freedom attached to that title.

Step VI
STEPPING TOWARDS EACH OTHER

The most awkward part after a marital storm is learning how to come back together. It feels a bit like someone having to re-teach you how to walk. It will feel difficult, your bones will feel shaky, you will feel clumsy, and you'll probably trip over each other's feet for a while. Give it time, and soon enough, you'll be running.

Chapter 13
Repairs after the Storm

Up to this moment, you have done a lot of work on yourself, which is good, because change always needs to start with me, and not pointing your finger at your spouse. Most of the time, even in your marriage, change doesn't start with we, it starts with me. Whether you are the person who feels responsible for this storm entering into your marriage, or you were the person hurt by a decision your spouse made, in getting to a place of making repairs, you both have to go through the work of looking at yourself to see the part you have played in your marriage in order to see the role you want to have in the marriage ahead.

In Family Therapy, we see a lot of families bring their teenager in to see a counselor and get help. Most families get surprised when we turn the focus into the family having an issue and not the identified teenager. In our homes, we are quick to blame the easiest target in the room which most of the time is the out of control, hormonal teenager. Everyone else isn't the problem, it is them, or so they think. Everyone in the family has a part to play in the struggles the teenager is facing, and everyone has a role they can play in the healing. It is wrong to send a teenager into counseling and expect them to gain healing in isolation and expect them to be the only person to change. A Family Systems approach to therapy teaches us that the system has to change. For a Systems-based counselor, growth for the family needs more than one person to change. So if the client wants the teenager to change, the Systems-based counselor would argue that the whole family system needs to change.

For your marriage, you could be attempting the same dilemma in wanting the marriage to change, but in asking that only one person do the changing. We would tell you that the problem is in your goal. When the goal is for a person to change, we put all our focus on one single person, but when the goal is for the marriage to change, we spread our focus onto all the parts of the marital system so that both spouses go through a transformation in an attempt to change the marital system.

In marriage counseling, and in any marital repair work, the same healthy mindset has to take place. When we get to the place of marital repair, it's time for the marital system to change, not just one person. You will connect as you both reflect on yourself, but there will be a bigger disconnect and more voids present in the marriage if the expectation is for only one person to change. Don't ever get to the place in your marriage that you don't believe that you are susceptible to the same sin and temptation that your spouse has engaged in. There is work, and an appreciation, and a level of transformation that needs to take place among you both.

Security Check

My children will never experience going to the airport and picking someone up directly at the gate. Baggage claim is as far as we can go to pick up a loved one from the airport. The security measures have gotten so thorough that only people getting on a flight can go in that far. My family just got back from a trip a few months ago, our first family trip on an airplane with all three children. As we handed the attendant our tickets with 7 minutes left until the plane left the ground we got a rude ticket attendant that angrily let us know "we almost left without you, you need to get here earlier". We got scolded with a few more statements from him. I was pretty exhausted at this point. We just finished the whole ordeal about waiting in the security check-in line, having to take off our shoes (which the kids don't have to, but of course, they want to take their shoes off because everybody else is doing it), then take out everyone's tablets, and laptop computers, and so on and so on. We might as well have unpacked our carry-on luggage in front of the huge line behind us, and did I mention it was only 6:30 in the morning. It took all our energy to pack and get everyone to the airport.

After finally making it through what felt like the entirety of our trip through the security check-in, of course, all three kids choose NOW that they HAVE to go to the bathroom. All kids 8 and under at this point, when they have to go to the bathroom, they have to go, the world stops for a potty-break, doesn't the airplane attendant understand this?

The security check-in process seems to get more and more exhaustive every time you get on a flight. But, the security teams do this for our benefit, and for the safety of everyone involved. Going through security puts us in a place where someone is less likely to bring a weapon on board that could be used to harm someone else. The process is working, making it harder and less common to find breaches taking place at the airport and on planes.

This experience got me thinking, what if we could do the same thing for our marriages? What if before we walked down the aisle on our wedding day, we had to go through a security check-in first so that we could acknowledge all the weapons and sensitivities we are bringing into this marital journey that could harm our spouse. Of course, we would confiscate all things likely to do harm and figure out a way to do something about them because our intent is never to harm the person we love.

What I hope you hear, is that your intent isn't a criminal offense against your spouse, but each of us walks down the aisle on our wedding day with some unmarked baggage that we were hoping would leave us at the security check-in station but somehow manages to make its way past the officer. We need to do for our marriages what seems to be working at the airport, taking more time to get to the gate so that we can protect the flight ahead.

Since we are already married, it is never too late to examine what we have already brought into the marriage, things there by our own doing, and some generational sins that need to be confiscated in a Ziploc baggy before we take any more steps forward.

The Influence of Upbringing

Some of the root causes of safety and insecurities brought into your marriage may not even be coming from your spouse; they are sensitivities from your upbringing. Your spouse may do something or have done something that hit an already sensitive nerve, but realizing where that scar first became a wound in your life is an important distinction to make. If you grew up in an environment that didn't feel safe and weren't able to practice communication skills in a healthy way we can bring that inexperience into our marriage. Both spouses need to be honest with recognizing what aspects of safety they are not getting from their spouse, and what are the needs for safety you desperately need because it is a longing on your soul that you have never experienced in your upbringing. As adults, when a childhood void gets met in adulthood, it creates an earthly peace that puts us in a place of sensitivity if the source is coming from an unhealthy outlet.

It is essential to be mindful of the danger in getting to a point where without asking, we are looking for our marriage or others to fulfill a need that was a void in our heart before we even got married. Your spouse needs to know those holes in your heart, and more importantly, you need to know them as well. These needs are aspects of your life that require extra attention from your spouse and an area you may want to consider working on individually.

Avoiding that you have needs can be unhealthy as well. I can certainly confess I've tried that path as well and didn't get very far.

As you start to think about your sensitivities, longings, and voids along with where they came from, you need to know that you may also struggle to feel those same voids in being secure in trusting your relationship with God. Said another way, the insecurities you are deeming only present in your marriage may be insecurities you feel in your relationship with your Maker.

Does God really have my best interest at heart?
Does God really care about me?
Does God really know me?
Does God really hear me when I cry out to him?

Sit in this one; you may not even realize the power of how not feeling safe in earthly relationships has a direct influence on not feeling safe being with God. If you look for security through the world first and God second it may skew the consistent response because our world is only consistent in being self-serving. Finding your answers for security can give you a broader window into where all of these voids are coming from, and are you turning to the right source of support to fill the void.

To dig into this deeper, ask yourself this question:

Have you been able to turn to God for help and healing more than any other person right now? Be honest with yourself. If not, what keeps you from fully feeling safe enough to make God the number one source of comfort through the storm you and your spouse have been walking through?

Repairs to your marriage need to be made with the guidance and counsel from your Creator. The one that began a good work in you will see your marriage into completion, into wholeness, with God's discerning Spirit as your guide. Don't make the mistake of trying to repair your marriage without repairing or starting a relationship with your Father. He will never stop chasing after you. Once He is invited in to do the repairs, this Master Builder can give you an estimate and begin helping you rebuild your marriage into something you could have never foreseen before all this.

Contributing Factors

After reflecting on accepting that sin has entered your marriage, experiencing a greater understanding of God's grace and healing on your soul, and seeking the redefinition and practice of forgiveness, you are ready to go back into your past. But only go backward in the safety of connecting everything back to how it impacts your today. If you go back and don't connect and apply that past to the present than all you are doing is going back. Why would you jump in a time machine if you weren't planning on doing anything while you were there? Present and Future application on lessons learned from our Past is the only way we can do something about our Past.

Some things led you and your marriage to be in a sensitive place during that season and put you in a position of vulnerability to sin. As crucial as recovering and repairing the damages of this storm has been, let's try and stay as clear as possible from having ever to take this trip through the desert again. Learning from the storm and doing something about those lessons is our huge takeaway when it comes to making repairs. This part of our journey is where we want to examine some of the root causes that led up to the sin. These are the things at the beginning of the book I encouraged you not to do on the front end because it is easy to fall in the trap of using contributing factors to blame your sin. Remember that we said to start this journey with ownership and not blame. But since you have done that, now let's go back, and if you are in a professional counseling setting, you may already be doing this in some of your sessions.

Your Discovery

What are your contributing factors? What led you into this storm, into a place of addiction, a place of raging anger, of lies, abuse, emotional neglect, infidelity, or you fill in the blank? Whatever your unfaithfulness has been that has led you astray foremost from your

God, and also from your marriage, you should be able to name it by now. So, let's figure out where the voids are in your life that brought down your defenses and put you into a place you never wanted to be. In the area of recovery, if you and your spouse are ready to hear one another, rebuilding your marriage will come from the intimate communication and connectedness that flows from these conversations.

/ / Exercise: Where did this come from? / /

1. Can you remember a time in your life where you struggled with this same sensitivity, or even witnessed someone in your life struggle with this issue?
2. What is the worst memory that comes to mind as you think about this struggle?
3. What does that memory say about you as a person?
4. When is the first and the most recent time or scenario in your life you remember feeling that way about yourself?
5. What would you prefer to believe about yourself as you look back on this?
6. Are there healthy outlets in your life that can help you feel about yourself the response you gave from question #5?

Gaining a better sense of contributing factors can empower you as your eyes can be on the lookout for future sensitivities. If the mind and our behaviors are connected, then you can be ready for the next attack. When you start to notice yourself in a situation that confirms whatever your response was to question #3, you will know that you have hit a sensitive trigger in your life, and a trigger that won't be resolved by turning to sin.

We need to hit these sensitivities head on. Your level of self-awareness will give you strength over your circumstances, and allow you to see even on the foggiest of days.

As you answered those questions, and as you continue to think through how to answer those questions, you are not alone. The next part of that exercise is whether you feel safe enough to talk to your partner about how you answered those questions. There is power in you both being united in understanding the contributing factors and susceptibilities in one another's lives, but communication and vulnerability require safety.

Safety

Time to make some examinations in the safety of your marriage. At this season of repair, we need to look at what was happening within your marriage that when you were going through a difficult time you weren't able to turn to your spouse for support, or maybe you did, and they didn't read the signals that you were screaming for help. Is your spouse someone that you can turn to when you are going through something difficult, or are they someone you already feel like a major disappointment too and admitting a struggle will only give them more ammunition for the condemning attacks on you?

Safety needs to be a goal. Safety needs to be a top priority in your marriage, and my first goal when I lead couples in a counseling room. Most of the time this is where we start with couples in marital therapy sessions. It is hard to do any repair if the two spouses are fighting the process of reconnection because they don't feel safe to turn towards their spouse. If your partner doesn't feel safe with you, it will be hard to turn towards one another the moment something is off in your marriage both now and in the future issues to come.

The people we love the most can often be the people we have hurt the most. Sad, but true, and that's not God's design for marriage or relationships. If there is something you are doing in your marriage that makes your partner not feel safe to come to you, you need to confess that and work at that sin in your heart. I know that trust is something you will have to build back, but you need to continually examine your heart to notice if you find yourself continually believing the best or the worst out of your spouse. Your heart and mind are connected more than you realize, and if you believe in your heart the worst out of them, then your mind and the way you treat them will be in line with your heart, and you may be treating them in a way that makes them not feel safe.

/ / Exercise: Define Safety / /

What does it look like for your partner to feel safe in your marriage? Greg Smalley asked 1,000 couples for help defining emotional safety in his book Fight your way to a Better Marriage (Smalley, 2012, p. 268-269) and the answers he received can help us learn if we are creating a safe place for our spouse and if they are in turn doing the same for us. Here were some of their responses for what safety in marriage is like (*Star the items you need the most, underline the things you need to work on practicing the most):

- Feeling completely secure
- Being accepted for who I am
- Feeling relaxed and comfortable
- Being free to express who I really am
- Being loved unconditionally
- Feeling respected
- Knowing that my spouse is trustworthy
- Having my spouse be there for me
- Being fully understood
- Being valued and honored
- Having loving reassurance
- Being able to open fully in order to give and receive love
- Not being judged
- Being seen for who I am
- Having my flaws accepted as part of the whole package
- Living in an atmosphere of open communication

Did any of these strike a chord with you? To complete this exercise, both of you use a different color pen and *star the ones on here that are the most important to you right now. This may change over time, but what are the ones you feel you need the most to be striving for as a goal at this sensitive place in the repair of your marriage. The other step I want you to take is with that same colored pen underline a couple of them that you know you need to work on doing a better job at expressing with your spouse. Remember that every aspect of repair in marriage is a balance of giving and taking where you both do your part at coming towards one another.

Chapter 14
Rebuild after the Storm

By this point, you have been through a lot, and the roller coaster of emotional experiences you have had to go through has been tougher than you thought possible. The weight of depression, anxiety, shame, blame, anger, and guilt have created ups and downs in your life that may have felt like you just hiked Mount Everest.

However you handled this journey, know that going through this process the right way will be worth more than gold. The priceless lessons you have learned about yourself, your spouse, your marriage, and your relationship with Christ are invaluable at this point. The world should look a bit different now, not because it has changed, but because you have. Hopefully, one day, you can use your experiences to disciple someone else in your life as you walk alongside their darkest moments. But before you get there, we still have more things to learn as we rebuild a foundation with your spouse.

Unconditional Love

One of the best goals in your marriage is striving and working towards an unconditional love for one another. I know you might think that unconditional love is supposed to come naturally, but in some relationships, it is a lesson we have to learn and practice over time. In a marriage, for instance, there is a form of conditional love that parenthood doesn't seem to have.

Parenthood seems to have an ingrained love for our kids that is almost genetically wired to be unconditional. In the way I view my kids, they can do nothing so wrong that it keeps me from loving and believing the best in them and their future. My love for them doesn't change based off of their mood. My mood may change, but my love remains constant for them. To stress this with my kids, I will tell them in their moodiest, crankiest, and brattiest moments that "even when you are grumpy Mommy still loves you". I overemphasize this statement with my kids, so they know that I fundamentally and foundationally love them.

My love for them is not dependent upon their mood or their character. I just love them. My love for them has no expectations, requirements, or standards. Now, my hope for them in life has expectations, requirements, and standards, but not my love. My love, they get freely, not based upon any grades, conduct, sickness, moodiness, or roller coaster emotions. They wake up loved by me and fall asleep loved by me. This truth is a constant I want them to know in their life. No matter what happens when they leave their bed each day, they carry my love with them. As they grow into adolescence and adulthood, my prayer is that this level of unconditional love they connect to how their God cares for them even more than I am able to. This is my heart for my kids, a heart that comes so naturally and easy for me, but even a love that feels natural with our kids may need to be practiced when it comes to our spouse.

This level of unconditional love becomes hard to do with adults. There may even be wiring in our brains that is present with our kids that just isn't there with other people in the world. Conditional love seems to be more prevalent among adult and marital relationships than we realize. You might not have even known that your love was conditional until your marriage suffered a crisis. In a state of crisis, our brain goes straight to the until-sin-do-us-part mindset where we begin to research what the legal requirements in our state are for getting a divorce. We even make a quick "pro" and "con" list in our head to decide if this is worth sticking out. A fresh start or a "do-over" seems like the perfect answer when the safety in your marriage has been jeopardized.

The back door may be your initial instinct when a storm blows through, but take note that when we are quick to find the back door to our marriage, we need to fully think through whether the love we share in our relationship is conditional or unconditional. When your marriage has the initial tendency to hit the back door, or one or both of you throw around the "D" word (divorce) on a regular basis or during every verbal bash, this is an easy sign that there is a breach of safety in your marriage. Threatening to leave because you aren't getting perfection is a great example of making your spouse feel conditionally cared for and makes them hesitant to share their current and future struggles with you.

Can I Love Them Again?

After working through safety and learning any tendencies or breaches to be aware of, it's time to work on regaining love after the pain of sin has surfaced in your marriage. Finding love after a struggle, and even learning to love in the middle of a struggle is one of those things I am not sure how secular couples make it through. Without an understanding of God's heart, love, and grace towards us, complete healing seems unbearable. When we look at the actual divorce rate, there isn't a significant difference between the divorce rate among people who go to church and couples who don't. That understanding poses so many questions for me. The assumption would be that Christians that have a different view of love and forgiveness would have marriages that could make it through a crisis together. That would be the assumption, but the reality is that Christian or not, our human nature struggles with love and forgiveness.

Can you imagine the radical shift that would take place if the character of Christ and his message of selfless relationships was so central among the marriages in our churches that even the sermons we heard had more to do with understanding how to love the people in our house than only starting with loving our neighbors? The process of selfless love begins with the people under the same roof as us, and even the people in the same church as us. When we start the journey of finding love in a place it feels lost, we need to start with ourselves and recognizing that our love should have never wavered. The way we love and the way we forgive should be what stands out in our marriages, that sets us apart from the divorce rate among people outside the church. Our marriages should stand out in the way we love beyond deserving and forgive without fully understanding.

Finding love again starts by redefining what it is you are looking for. If you are looking to find-love-again, you are already at the wrong starting line. Re-Defining-Love needs to be the goal. What you had is never the goal you should want to achieve. We are children of a God that makes things New, why would you want to go back when there is something more in store for what is up ahead. I hope you have positive memories and thoughts of good times together that serve as the strength for a positivity that is to come, but getting the past back isn't the goal of rebuilding love.

We are reforming into a new creation from what's existing, and just like a piece of clay can turn into many forms, the substance remains the same, a piece of clay. No matter the shape it forms into, it is still just a piece of clay. Limitless possibilities, but the material doesn't change. The ball that started before you has so much potential, that why would our striving ever be to return as the ball that started on the table.

In the potter's hands, our marriage can turn into something beautiful. We will remain in the same bodies and be the same people but will be refined into a beautiful creation. That's our hope in redefining how to love each other, its relearning love to a deeper degree than we understood it before this crisis entered our lives. What beauty we have in this shift of perspective that some people won't get this blessing of suffering to understand? (gulp, still hard to say the blessing of suffering, but I know it's true) To learn what it means to love through grace is a discipline of love that teaches us what it means to love with the image of Christ at heart.

Meaningful Changes

In your search to relearn how to love, you first need to understand love, and maybe you're doing this for the first time. You may have never received a good form of premarital counseling or parental example that helped you define love to see if you both were even on the same page before you said, "I do". Crazy that we can say "I do" to each other without first defining what it is we are agreeing too. Any legal institution would make sure all parties agree to the terms before you put down any signatures, but many couples tend to say "I do" to being married faster than we say "I do" to understanding what love in marriage actually means.

Doing a check-in before marriage to make sure you are both on the same page with how you define and describe your relationship isn't the only time this is important. Not only do I believe in some form of premarital therapy before marriage, but my recommendation to couples is that they do some type of marital check-in at each meaningful change of their marriage. Getting married is just the first meaningful change we take as a couple, but there are many more that come right on the heels after exchanging rings. (1) Making it through the first 3 years is closing the door on being newlyweds and needing a check-in at all you have discovered in your first couple of years together; then (2) having kids is a redefinition of learning what it means to gain the titles "mom" and "dad" without losing the titles, "husband" and "wife". There are even more meaningful changes: major moves; job changes; even learning to go from a working mom to a stay-at-home mom; then the phase of raising hormonal teenagers (which changes the entire dynamic, smell, and energy level in the house); becoming empty nesters, and one-day retirement are both time periods that need a whole redefinition on your purpose and significance in life. These meaningful changes are all transitional periods that will shape our character and teach us major lessons in our life. These periods will be pivotal times in our life where we will either turn closer to God and our spouse or turn away. The battle of the Spirit and the flesh will take place at every meaningful change in our life, which is why we have to do a check-in, to remind us to center back in. Each of these meaningful changes needs intentionality on drawing closer to God, and our spouse or else the stage of life will become the priority and the relationship will get put on pause, and we will forget or become too tired to ever go back to the remote and press the play button.

Continual check-ins throughout your marriage are vital as you are now learning the reality that during significant shifts in the life of your marriage you go through growth spurts and 'change' spurts. Your self-development and that of your spouse have times where changes occur. Changes where the person you married is different than the person you married. This stranger we become married to we have to learn how to love. Tim Keller goes through this in more length on his chapter on Loving the Stranger in his book with his wife The Meaning of Marriage. He gives us insight on our relationship with our spouse being that of learning a stranger. What happens over time is that "marriage changes us, having children changes us, a career switch changes us, age changes us.

On top of everything else, marriage brings out and reveals traits in you that were there all along but were hidden from everyone including you, but now they are all seen by your spouse" (Keller, 2011, p. 147). This thought helps us define love as a process of learning love; this is the reason behind its verb pretense. It is an action, something you are acquiring, a process, a journey. It will uncover things about you that lurked quietly in the shadows during your courtship.

It reminds me of the love I have for my children. When they were infants, I loved them beyond imagine. But they were different then, without much of the personality and individual uniqueness I see in them today. I loved them when they were pure, and innocent, good, and to me, perfect. At each developmental stage, I have a similar but different kid with new needs and desires for love and affection. There was a time when I rocked them to sleep, there was a time they wanted a never-ending back rub to fall asleep to, and a time when a kiss and hug goodnight was all they wanted to feel my affection before bed. Much like their needs changing, I had to adapt to the person with a bigger shoe size standing in front of me (and almost taller than me).

With Matt, he has changed so much over our marriage, and so have I. Our pictures look almost identical, but our inner growth has been influenced by the major life transitions we are exhausted but blessed from going through over the years. Our expression of love and even thoughts about each other need to mature and shift as we as people do. It amazes me how the things that come naturally to us in the way we love our kids takes a tremendous amount of effort in learning how to care for our spouse.

Keller goes on to give us a new charge for loving our spouse:

> "What if, however, you began your marriage understanding its purpose as spiritual friendship for the journey to the new creation? What if you expected marriage to be about helping each other grow out of your sins and flaws into the new self God is creating? Then you will actually be expecting the 'stranger' seasons, and when you come to one you will roll up your sleeves and get to work" (Keller, 2011, p. 149).

What a great depiction of the result and action of love, especially in learning how to love through the experience and even expectation of weakness. This is where we are at in our marital journey, rolling up our sleeves and getting to work. We are learning this stranger in combination with learning how to love them.

Identity

Let's continue looking at love, real love, not fairy tale love, the real stuff. Real love is going to be the pouring on of concrete in rebuilding our marriage, and we have to do that by first looking at our vertical relationship with our God. We start there more than just because it is the bible school answer, we start with our loving relationship with God because it is the secret to putting him in the middle of repairing and regaining a loving relationship with the spouse that you have hurt or been hurt by. We have to start with acknowledging that there is a third party in the marriage, one that has probably not been recognized to the level He needs to be. God is a part of the covenantal relationship in your marriage, and understanding His love for you as a son or daughter of Christ means also looking to the person sitting next to you, or the person you are separated from right now and seeing them as a child of God too.

Can you do that for me? Can you recognize that the same person that has been disobedient in loving you, has also been disobedient in fully loving God? Can you realize that the spouse that has been yelling and frustrated at you is a son or daughter of God? Can you acknowledge that the protective parent in our God sees their sin but still unconditionally loves them and is watching the way you are treating His child?

The road ahead and even up to this point is difficult to do if you can't look at your spouse as a child of God. If you are the only child of God and your spouse is a spawn of the devil you are going to struggle to love them with the heart that God has desired for your marriage.

Love is more than a word, it is a verb, an action, a process that we learn the deeper we get. The more I understand my Father's love for me the more I realize how undeserving I am of it. When I look at my spouse, I want to think the same way. The more I realize the blessing and gift my husband is to me, my kids, and what he brings into this world, the more I realize how undeserving I am that this imperfectly perfect man belongs to me.

Entitlement will reverse the order, especially when sin enters in. Entitlement's voice will tell you that they should be thankful you are choosing to stay, and love says that you are still lucky to be with them, despite everything.

Prayer

Prayer is the best avenue for restoring our lives and shifting our heart and even flourish in the way you love your spouse. I know your response, you're about to skip this section because your thinking "I'm not a prayer person, it just feels weird and so one-sided". If you had that quick response to prayer, I might even tell you that it may play a part in the reason you were so sensitive when tempted towards sin to begin with and will be your downfall again if you don't figure out this important spiritual discipline in your life. I won't ever tell you that the best way to connect with your spouse is to solely believe that you are married and cross your fingers hoping it works out. Instead, I would ask that you spend time with them, talk to them, listen to their heart. The same becomes true as you use the Holy Spirit to intercede for you as you communicate with your Father.

You need to pray to have a relationship with your Father, and you need to pray about the things on your heart. Hopefully on your heart is your marriage and your family. To be the best model for them of what it looks like to be a son or daughter is to be obedient and have a relationship with your Heavenly Father. If you want to rebuild your marriage into something beautiful, don't just pray; pray on your knees, pray in the shower, pray on your drive to work, sneak into your kid's room and pray over them while they sleep. Let prayer envelop your heart and your life because prayer is a form of our worship and praise to our Father. Talk to him. You do your loved ones a complete disservice by not praying for them and your heart towards them. Your God loves hearing your voice, and when you don't know what to say, listen, sit with him and listen. You might even hear something.

One of the best things I hear come out of Matt's mouth is when he tells me something that God is teaching him or showing him.

There is nothing that makes me feel more connected to him than to hear that God is alive in his life. As you restore love for your spouse, the best prayer is that you continually ask God to help you see your spouse the way He does. Over and over, can you look at that sinner and say that he/she was worth Jesus dying on a cross for? Your Father sees that, so pray that you can see it too.

Coming Together

Going through this crisis in your marriage, what decisions did you make? I know I told you at the beginning not to make any major decisions, but you probably made some, you may have made some before you even bought this book. Maybe you guys haven't been sleeping in the same room, or you decided to separate because you couldn't stand the sight of the person that hurt you. You may be living in the house together but are roommates more than soul mates. The silent treatment may have turned into a survival ritual where there is a complete void of communication.

It's time to come back together slowly. If you have decided that you want to rebuild your marriage, let's do this one brick at a time. Find something to talk about that doesn't revolve around the pain and trauma you have been going through. Your life and marriage are bigger than this storm. Be careful not to make going through this awful weather the only thing you talk about. It will hurt every time. You still need to talk about it, and great connectedness will come from these emotionally tough conversations, but if it is all you talk about it is harder to come together. Find safe places and times where you both talk through the pain and recovery you are going through, but venting all day through texts that feel like you are getting shot by a bullet every time your phone beeps isn't the best path for coming together. Remember that safety will help bring you steps closer. Violence and threats, whether directly or indirectly, verbal or nonverbal are steps you take away from each other.

Coming together can be a bit of a slow process, one that is very much dependent on whether the flame with your spouse was completely extinguished, or if a small fire remained throughout the trials in recovery. Each situation will look different as you move towards one another, just know that right now any movement towards is a movement to be celebrated. Dr. John Gottman is highly respected in the therapeutic community for his work and study on relationships. In his book, The Seven Principles for Making Marriage Work, he talks about the spouses beginning to turn towards one another by explaining how:

> "One virtue of turning toward each other is that it is so easy to accomplish. It only takes a small gesture to lead to another and then another. 'Turning toward' operates under a law of positive feedback – like a snowball rolling downhill, it can start small yet generate enormous results. In other words, you don't have to turn to your partner in a dramatic way to see the benefit. Just get started, and things will improve by themselves" (Gottman & Silver, 1999, p. 89).

We cannot build the marriages we long for and that God desires for us if our backs are towards each other with arms crossed. We must turn around, face the person we are learning to love and take one step at a time. Just like any accurate weight loss program, the people with the long-term weight loss success stories are the people who made one step at a time towards making healthy decisions that were good for their bodies and not bad. Applying a healthy lifestyle consistently is the key. Your marriage will slowly start to look different, keep at it, stay consistent in moving towards one another and long-term results will show a new picture when you both look in the mirror. It's not easy to change your lifestyle and make decisions that are against your normal habit, but it can be done, and it will result in a healthier, happier, and holier way to be in a relationship with your spouse.

// Exercise: Something to look forward to. //

It's hard to see the future right now, it may even be harder to think about next week. But you saw a future with this person, you both had dreams of things you wanted to accomplish and places you one day wanted to go together. Remember that those dreams aren't lost. You feel like you've lost everything, but you haven't. You lost the story that the person that loved you would never hurt you, or that you would be the perfect spouse you had hoped. That ideal image may have been what you've lost, but in actuality, that expectation for your marriage was probably higher in your mind than it should have been. Maybe you feel like the only thing you learned was that you keep getting hurt by the person who says they love you. God is the author of all stories, and his penmanship is eloquent and inspiring. He can write a different ending from this than what the world scripts out what "next" is supposed to look like. Invite God in, surrender your marriage to Him and see how He writes the next chapter.

Thinking of the future can remind you of a piece of hope. For Matt and I, we have been married 12 years, and we hold on to the hope that the next 12 years we can love each other through the lessons we learned from the past. Your past can't be changed, if I figure out a way to do that, you'll be the first to know, cause boy am I working on a way to do that. Until my time machine starts to work, can you write out some of the dreams you and your spouse had before all of this (maybe a vacation spot, a house, a business you wanted to start together...). There was a before all this, and keep in mind there will be an after all this too, trust me. List out some of the dreams you had before going through this crisis that are dreams that haven't been lost. You haven't lost everything.

_____

_____

_____

_____

Physical Space

There are more steps to take in coming together. Just physical presence is a big one. Are you in separate houses? Try being in the same house again, as long as you are in a position of being safe with one another. Is the TV on? Could you try sitting just a little closer on the couch? Has it been a while since you held your spouse's hand, or kissed them before they walked out the door? When it comes to physical presence, every person's story is going to be unique and different as far as where you both are at and what you feel comfortable or ready for. So, all I am asking is that whatever place you are at with physical presence in your marriage right now, could I encourage you to kick it up just one notch.

/ / Exercise: Appreciating your Spouse / /

Looking at your partner and seeing anything positive is a hard thing to do when you can't see past that sin-stained shirt they are wearing. This is where I want you to get out your journal or a sheet of paper, or open up the notes section on your smartphone. Every day find one thing you appreciate about your spouse, about their character and who they are. This isn't a pros and cons list where you are trying to decide whether to stay. I want you to begin the process of seeing beauty in a place you have been struggling to see anything good. You may find yourself struggling with this task a bit. I put a list of character words in the resource section of this book to help you think of actual character traits that your partner possesses. They are special and unique, they are a child of God, full of worth and value and when you pray that God gives you His lens to look at your spouse, you will see that God sees a man and woman full of amazing character and potential.

Dating.

Have you been on a date yet? My husband and I's first time out after one of our major storms felt like the eye of the storm. It was calm and quiet but was awkward and uncomfortable. It felt like there was a whole new part of the storm ahead. We had to redefine who we were, or at least carefully examine it in a way we had never done before.

We were hoping we could stay out for a while, at least until my sister had our kids asleep, but our moods spiraled into a negative place. We ended up just wanting dinner to get over with so that we could go home. We weren't fighting with each other at that moment, it's just hard to get back to a normal life and be surrounded in a public setting as if everything is the same when you know in your heart that nothing is the same anymore. We weren't starting completely over, we just had to relearn our relationship and gain a deeper understanding of each other. There are also going to be good days, and some bad days, the hope for beginning to date each other right now is for more good days than bad ones.

Our next date night went ok, we made it through the dinner and enjoyed being out together, but then the conversation took a turn, and my waterworks started flooding before we could pick up the check to leave. We weren't waiting until it was easy to start going out on dates together, we were able to maturely admit that it is going to be a process and will be hard for a while, but we both have the same goal of getting to a place where it isn't uncomfortable anymore. Getting through these awkward, difficult, and uncomfortable conversations is just a part of the path to healing.

A great encouragement during these uncomfortable moments in your relationship is to remember that you have survived many awkward moments in your marriage leading up to this. After learning the realities of what it means to adequately care and survive the first year of raising a baby we somehow managed to make the conscious decision to do it two more times. Even today, when our house is pure chaos with everyone, well, being themselves, Matt and I have a saying that puts a smile on our faces, we look at each other, and say, "three kids was such a great idea, I am glad we had three". Of course, there is sarcasm in our voice, but it is filled with truth as well. Getting through those baby and toddler stages were rough, getting through the pregnancies were rough, but we went through the tough times because we saw the long-term value in getting through the difficult stages of parenthood. The blessings at the other end far outweigh the awkward struggles.

We need to look at our marriages, and right now dating and communicating in the same way. It's weird right now, and you are going through a bit of a weird puberty stage in your marriage at this point. This puberty stage is completely awkward, and a bit ugly, but that pimple face grew up and is handsome or beautiful today. Sometimes we have to go through the acne stage until we get to an age where our skin evens out. Our marriages do the same thing. This is just your acne story as you get back into dating. It will smooth over, just keep at it. Don't quit just because it's hard. Living your life that way will never build your character. Real character is built facing the challenges and breaking through the difficult encounters.

Keep going out on date nights until you find that each one gets better than the one before. One Lego brick at a time, but you have to start with the Legos in a bunch of scrambled pieces on the table before you end up with that awesome Star Shooter.

Chapter 15
Proactive for the Storms Ahead

Flat Tires

Flat tires are the worst. They never come when they are expected, and they aren't exactly ever expected. A tire is a hefty expense when you think of all the things in your budget for the month that are still in the "need" category. With school just starting back up, my kids need a new pair of shoes, all three kids, and they each could use more than one pair. My son that grows an inch every week needs me to take him to grab a few pairs of jeans. They are also due for needing their next yearly well visit to the doctor. I haven't even started on the to-do projects piling up with a cost attached to them in the house.

Even though the things-to-do right now are bigger in this season than the financial budget can do, here I sit in an empty parking lot with a flat tire trying to sort out how to add this Flat Tire to the list. The shoes and the health visits are going to have to wait because in the immobilization I am experiencing in this moment, getting a new tire has been bumped to the top of the list.

Before we figure out a way to solve today's uninvited chaos I am sitting here in my car just processing all this out. Through the many storms we have walked through in our life, we are learning that even when the weather is beautiful, and the rain has just lifted, even on those days there will come a flat tire. I called Matt to tell him where I am and asked if he could meet me. His first response is exactly how we have been feeling in our life right now, "well, when it rains it pours".

One minute I am driving down the road utterly smooth sailing and within a matter of three minutes I am side-parked after a glass bottle just flew out of the car in front of me and landed right in front of the car and shattered as I heard the glass crumble under my front left tire.

Really? Really? There is someone who literally just kept on driving going about his/her day without realizing that I am parked and stranded and 100% immobile and about to be out $200 because something flew out of your car. They will suffer no consequence from today, and we will pay out of our budget for the expense of a mistake I didn't make other than being on the road.

This is the experience I am having right here as I sit typing away in my car, and the experience that has tangibly played itself out in different seasons of our marriage. We can be smooth sailing, cruising down the road as if it were any other day in our life, and all of a sudden a flat tire comes in and completely inconveniences our marriage. On some occasions (and there have been more than one), I am entirely to blame. I am not focusing and turn onto a curb just a little too quickly, and on other days, like today, I am now having to play an active role in fixing a situation that is in front of me that isn't my fault.

Have you ever felt that way or been put in a situation where you had to deal with a problem that shouldn't be your problem? And even bigger than that, you may be in a spot right now in your marriage where you feel that "when it rains, it pours".

As we plan ahead for a proactive marriage and proactive maintenance on our vehicles, some things are just going to come up. Even if the oil changes and inspections are all up to date, there will be days where the wheels will be completely out of alignment. Even days where the radiator will go out. We have already gone through seasons where we questioned whether the tires in our marriage were actually the problem, and debated if we should just call the car completely totaled.

Today, the car is fixable. In the grand scheme of today, this feels awful, but in the grand scheme of our lives, this flat tire is just a rainy day compared to the storm explosions of car troubles we have had to go through in our past.

Our marriage is not much different than the maintenance of our vehicles. We want to set up a proactive future prepared for the best days of our marriage yet to come but also ready for the unexpected flat tires that throw us off course as we make our way back.

Each step we take now is hopefully one that is moving us towards one another in our marriages. We may not have reached the goal we have been striving towards, but we need to remember this is a process more than it is a destination. As our marriages go through this growth spurt, we now need to refocus on being proactive with our present relationship to avoid having to be only reactive in the future. At this point, we can do all of this through the knowledge and experience we have gained from going through the trials we have endured in the past. When the past continually repeats itself, we gain patterns in our life that need to be addressed and dealt with appropriately.

When we look back on the hardships and trials we have been through together let's consider again the impact of a devastating storm that had catastrophic effects on the city it blew through. The aftermaths of a storm require the provision of immediate safety, caring for the needs of the hurt and displaced, rebuilding the place of impact, and preparing for the next surprise attack to be met with a stronger and more strategized environment.

The key to making it better is realizing that you could not fully know how the town would stand against a category 4 hurricane unless the town went through one. Once it has, the strength can be formed from the experience it witnessed. The town now has tangible results for where the water was rising and how the houses and electrical cables held up during the storm. The town has a decision to make. They can rebuild through only repairing the damage that was caused, or they can repair with intentionally and make the area stronger than it was before.

My observation: the smart city's learn from what has happened and rebuild hoping that the same lessons don't have to be learned twice. Our marriage observation is the same. Now that we have gone through catastrophe, now that we have witnessed the house being flooded, and the trees shattering our roofs, we can now rebuild with a stronger framework in mind.

Moving in Circles

Without new insight, after all we have been through in our marriage, we are subject to living our marriage moving in circles rather than moving forward. This is not the way we were meant to live. We were meant to live in forward motion. We were meant to live learning the lessons from the generation before us. We were meant to live with a hopeful tomorrow in mind. If not, your life will feel like a hamster spinning on a wheel without actually going anywhere.

God's design for you was more than that of a hamster, and if it weren't, you would have been created as a hamster. The definition of your life has a bigger meaning. The lessons you learn at the critical moments you have been through can accentuate on God's strength or highlight your weakness. Even better, you can learn how to accentuate God's strength through your weakness. As God is glorified through this storm, let the light shine through the growth you both have endured. Now is when we go forward in our marriage with the proactive instinct that we may not have had or applied before all of this. Now is when we can look ahead and put into practice techniques and skills that can prevent us from getting back on the hamster wheel.

Ephesians

It's rare to hear a talk or see a marriage book that doesn't mention Ephesians 5:21-33 where we learn how a husband and a wife are to treat each other. The way that I have framed this book is the way I counsel couples in marital therapy and the structure that I see laid out in the book of Ephesians. Let me explain since you've stayed with me for this long. You deserve to know why I started so lengthy talking about "you" before I went into the "us". Most people start with a speech right at the 21st verse of chapter 5 in Ephesians, but it's hard to start there when there are significant verses from 5:1-20. The first half of chapter 5 doesn't talk about our relationship with our spouse, it paints a picture of who we are to be in our relationship with God and begins in verse one acknowledging that placement as being "dearly loved children" (5:1) of God, and that we are supposed to live according to being His child. That we are to be "children of the light" (5:8), and become "filled with the Spirit" (5:18).

I could even go into depth with you at the verses that end Ephesians chapter 4, reminding us that we have "put off your old self, which is being corrupted by its deceitful desires; to be made new in the attitude of your minds; and to put on the new self, created to be like God in true righteousness and holiness" (4:22-24). These are all pivotal verses that come prior to the common knowledge verses in Ephesians 5 about "wives, submit to your husbands as to the Lord" (5:22) and "husbands, love your wives, just as Christ loved the church and gave himself up for her" (5:25).

I don't believe you get the whole picture if you don't first start with yourself and your relationship with God, and Paul knew that when he wrote this letter and didn't start with the Husband and Wife relationship but led up to it. We spent a lot of time there right at the beginning of this book. It is no coincidence to me that before our famous Ephesians 5 verses is the charge to "not let any unwholesome talk come out of your mouths, but only what is helpful for building others up according to their needs, that it may benefit those who listen…Get rid of all bitterness, rage, and anger, brawling and slander, along with every form of malice. Be kind and compassionate to one another, forgiving each other, just as in Christ God forgave you." (Ephesians 4:29-32)

Stick with me, this all has to do with building a proactive marriage.

After reading those verses, I feel it is impossible to be proactive in our marriage if we undermine the work Christ has to do in ME so that I can accomplish how he asks me to treat Matt for the rest of today and tomorrow. I am not perfect, and I will miss the mark probably every day, but I am trying, and I want to follow the verses before chapter 5:21 so that I can do 5:21-33 appropriately.

That is the design for how I counsel couples and for the format of this book. We have to start with God's commands for the way I am to live my life so that my lens for how I treat my husband through my disobedience to him or even his disobedience to me can be filtered through the way God wants us to love and treat other people. The verses before chapter 5:21-33 are what will give us the shift to be the people our marriages need us to be to treat that relationship like it is sacred. There are times in a counseling room where I may spend more time on the verses leading up to than I do on the overused verses of 5:21-33.

Walking through this storm, and heading through these pages, we have done just that. We have spent the bulk of our time examining ourselves, our hearts, and being stripped by getting rid of the things that are "improper for God's holy people" (Ephesians 5:3). Now we can spend time looking ahead and applying principles that will help us be proactive in caring for the other person in our marriage with a Christ-like heart.

Intentionality

You are no stranger to the destruction and consequences associated with sin. At this point in the book, we have all become aware of the danger that walking down this dark alley has cost our lives and the turmoil it has put on the people we love around us. Step one in living a proactive marriage is to add intentionality to the vocabulary of your relationship.

If you are reading this and have ever walked into my counseling room, it is not new for you to hear me use the word "intentionality". I love this word so much because I see the intense amount of value it adds to our lives. We all add intentionality about the areas in our life that are important to us. We give extra focus and attention to the things that we prioritize and believe add value to our livelihood. Our marriage needs to be a thing that we see as adding value to our lives. Being married is more than a cultural expectation, it adds blessing to a self-centered world and shows us a bigger perspective of what it means to live outside of ourselves.

If you're asking how to be intentional in your marriage, I've got an answer. Bringing intentionality means to (1) go against the natural; to (2) be above average; and to (3) seek out ways to show that you care. This is just my definition, so you can understand where I am coming from. Let me break it out a little further:

(1) Go Against the Natural – Intentionality is not a part of our fleshly nature. Our instinct is self-preservation and self-care. It is a foreign concept that we have to teach the wiring in our brains to add space for. Thinking outside of yourself is not ingrained in your flesh, but will be a fruit that comes from the inclusion of aligning with the Holy Spirit. God's heart is intentional for all His children so a shift will happen as you go against the natural and conform to the heart of your Creator.

(2) Be Above the Average – Is there a place in your life where making average is just good enough for you? Maybe you felt this way in school, or in cleaning the house, cooking, or at work. You might see people who want perfection in one of those areas, but you are just fine with average work. We

are content with average in areas of our life that we don't prioritize.

Now marriage should be something we prioritize because we see its importance and significance in our lives. This relationship will last longer than our time living at home with our parents, and it will outlive the time we spend with our kids. It shouldn't be treated like we are ok with getting a 'B' or 'C' average, we should strive to be above average in our connectedness and ways we love and care for our spouse.

(3) Seek out ways to show you Care – Intentionality means to "seek out". Great marriages don't just happen. There, I just summed up the grand secret to every marriage on the face of our planet. It takes work and effort. It doesn't just happen. And if your marriage isn't great, that doesn't mean you should get a divorce to find a great one. It doesn't work like that. We have to seek out ways to show we care and tell the other person they are cared for. Without this, we tend to make assumptions, or we tend to get complacent. We assume our spouse knows we love them, we assume they feel appreciated, valued, and we assume they know that if we had to choose all over again today, we would still choose to say "I do" to them. A one-day wedding commitment isn't enough for your spouse to know you care about them, we have to find ways to show we care every day.

Useless Words

There is a great icebreaker game where you put the name of a celebrity on a name tag and go around the room putting the name tags on the backs of your friends. The point of the game is to guess which name is on your back, and for you to guess the person in front of you can give you descriptions and clues to help you guess the character on your back. After playing this game a lot in small church groups, business settings, and through volunteer trainings I started realizing the real-life version of this game that gets played more at my house than I want it to. At home, I see the tendency to reverse the order of this game. My husband and I are wearing our name tags on the front of our shirts, and we are learning information about ourselves through what is said about us and how we are treated by the people around us every day. It's almost a game where you learn the words used to describe you based on how people talk and treat you.

Words are a powerful tool in our toolbox, one so powerful in fact that if we misuse it, we can give a shattered image of identity to our spouse. Our words could be the next tornado storm that breaks the house into pieces.

When we use useless, hurtful words, we are in a sense trying to remind the person we love of the viewpoint they already have about themselves. At times, the harshest part is when we say words with a harmful intent and our words knock their view of themselves further down than it was before. There is power in words, and power even to destroy when we speak with useless words that gain nothing but hurt.

Let's commit to try and see what is going on here. At our core, we all have a nametag on our shirts, and we go about our days trying to figure out (1) if we have worth; (2) if we measure up; (3) if we are loved; and (4) if we are valued as part of our descriptions. Wouldn't it be great to be able to say a confident "yes" that you feel that way about those four things? Instead, we may think it temporarily or never at all seeking the validation we need from the world to instill whether or not these four categories can be associated with our identity.

Hopefully it changes the way you look at interactions with your spouse when you realize they are learning who they are by the way you speak to them. We tend to be a bit more demeaning when we believe we tell them something wrong about themselves because we are trying to show them how they aren't the person they think they are.

Here's an example from our life: on Tuesday mornings every week, it's quite consistent that the trash needs to be out at the curb by 7 am. Yep, you know where I am going with this don't you, this story you know far too well. Matt has gone through a radical transformation in this area throughout our 12-year marriage so I can't knock him too much. What I want to bring up is the fact that the one week he does forget, by 8 or 9 am I have a desire to text or call him. For some reason I text it because it doesn't feel as hurtful I guess in a text. I want to tell him "You forgot to put the trash out this morning". After being married the length we have, we still have a lot more to learn. My husband does have moments where instead of keeping his thoughts to himself he will just let me know the reality of how something I said makes him feel. It doesn't happen often, but when it does, I log it in my brain, and I think the way he said it to me helps capture the way most of us feel.

His response to my text: "thanks for telling me that, I am at work now so there's nothing I can do about it, but thanks for letting me know that I messed up". There's a little sarcasm in there, but more importantly, there is honesty. If I let him know at 9 am while he is at work something he forgot to do 3 hours earlier, then it's too late now for him to do anything about it. All I have done is made myself feel better (as if it is a part of my job description as his wife to say "hey you missed this deadline, this is going to go on your quarterly review"), and he doesn't want to hear that from me. He doesn't want to start a workday already feeling like he's failed for the day.

Our words have more merit than we think, in moments like those I find myself saying things just to say them, without realizing that Matt is shaping parts of his identity around the clues and facts I give him. That morning, the word "failure" he associated with himself and the nametag he wore the rest of the day.

He also likes to remind me that I tend to mention the one thing he forgot to do and not the five things he remembered to do, which probably influenced him forgetting that one thing in the first place. We have to be careful that we aren't highlighting the useless words while skipping over some productive ones.

/ / Exercise: Tell your Spouse they have Meaning / /

What words do you want your spouse to learn about themselves by the way you talk to them?

Any good company you work for is going to either ask for your goals, or they will give you goals and assess your attempt to reach them. Start to look at the way you talk to your spouse and think about the words you hope they know about themselves, you can start with the four we talked about earlier: (1) Worthy; (2) Measured Up; (3) Loved; (4) Valued.

- How can you affirm these traits in your spouse by the words you say to them this week?
- Can you rethink about your Spouses self-reflection to be something that is shaped by your responsibility?
- Can you make the way you talk to your spouse a goal you're striving to accomplish in your speech?
- How are you talking to your spouse?
- What traits do you hope your spouse is learning about themselves because of the reminders and words you speak to them?

Punishment of Reminders

Learning how to have a proactive marriage means finding the balance between forgiving and forgetting. I watched the comedian Jim Gaffigan the other night who talked about his wife saying that "she has the gift of being able to remember everything I have ever done wrong", "she is great at forgiving, she just doesn't forget". We tend to feel like that sometimes. We feel like even when we get to a place where we are healing and moving past a hurt, the person that sleeps beside you seems to be dreaming about how you hurt them at night to help them never move on or forget. Jim Gaffigan goes on to talk about the difference between forgiving and forgetting. He mentions the attempted assassination of Pope John Paul II, how the Pope made a visit to this man in prison to forgive him, "but then he goes home". Gaffigan brings home a major point with laughter saying we wouldn't really know if the Pope forgave this man unless he had to live in the cell with the man that tried to kill him. When it is time to do the dishes as cellmates, that would be the true test. The Pope would get told, "it's your night to do the dishes", and we would see his level of forgiveness and forgetting. He could easily respond with, "I would do the dishes, but remember that time you tried to kill me, I don't think I should ever have to do the dishes again".

This is an actual reality for what happens in most of our homes if we aren't careful. Behind the walls, we don't see the jabs each couple throws at each other. We practice the principle of forgiveness, but our actions don't show forgiveness, they show a life sentence. The way we treat our spouse after they have done something to hurt us is to condemn them with the punishment of reminders. "I'll stay with you, but don't expect me to forget", "remember, you owe me".

This way of thinking and responding is of the world, not of Jesus' teaching. Asking and receiving forgiveness is asked of us the same way our God gives it to us. We have to place ourselves in a position where the goal is to look at each other again, or for the first time, and be able to see past the wrongs they've done in the past. This is what it means to truly forgive and forget. Does the fact that this season was a part of your marriage go away…no? The transition comes in how you two choose to label this season of your life. You can choose to label this season as being defined by the constant reminders of the pain, or you can choose to label this season with the outcome of growth and the reminders of the growth that was birthed from that season. You'll have to think about that one, which choice do you think will bear peace as you have so much of your life up ahead.

Accountability

Getting caught in a sin is like driving a car. Everyone speeds, even though you might say you don't, we've all done it. We even have good excuses for it, "Running late for work", "About to have a baby", "Screaming kids in the car", the list can go on. The streets give us a clear, bold sign of the speed they deem is best for us to be driving, but we believe they are "more like guidelines than rules" (Bruckheimer, 2003). We take the speed limit sign as a suggestion more than a security put there for our safety, and in the secrecy of our car, when we do not see a police officer nearby, we do what we want and not what we are asked to do.

We speed, even if we rationalize that it is ok if it is only 5 or 10 miles over; that is still technically speeding. We drive at the rate we think is safe enough not to get caught. Not speeding isn't always your objective on the road, and being safe isn't always on your mind when you buckle your seatbelt when you're in a hurry to get somewhere, your primary goal becomes not getting caught speeding. While driving, the only thought and care are what we are allowed to do up to the line of getting caught. Then there's that moment when it happens. Your "luck" has run out, and you get a ticket. Oh, the weight of guilt! You don't feel guilty for all the times you have sped on that same street, just that today you got caught.

Soon after that, we drive more cautiously. The guilt causes a change and shift in our driving. We immediately see the reality of getting caught, and it frightens us enough for us to make a change, or at least change temporarily. Even through the experience of getting caught, we don't thoroughly learn our lesson as we aren't driving cautiously for our benefit or because we fully believe the rules are put there for our best interest. We drive the speed limit for a while after getting caught for fear of getting caught again.

In the middle of the storm there is guilt, and in recognizing the pain that sin has brought into our marriage, we also need to recognize the sin. Understanding fully what we have done so that we don't have to make this a regular occurrence when the guilt begins to wear off. Learning the disservice that sin brings to our lives and our marriages and how it distances us from our relationship with God needs to be the safety rail that helps this from recurring. Without a level of understanding, we run the risk of walking back into our sin the moment our guilt starts to fade. Much like speeding in your car again after getting a ticket. Once enough time has gone by, and you feel like you are safe from getting caught again, you jump back into going 10 miles over.

Let's not make this storm a pattern in our lives.

A perfect storm story may have leading factors that got you both here, but we don't want this to become a groundhog experience that gets relived over and over again.

There is so much more that is ahead for your marriage, so much that is even coming now through this storm. Don't let the fear of getting caught be the only guardrail to not allowing sin have a foothold in your life, find support and resources that remind you to turn to the truth before you get intertwined in a new web of lies.

The future for your marriage can look bright, no matter what you are thinking or even what your friends are saying in your ear, the light ahead can be brighter than you realized or anyone around you is expecting. We have talked a lot about forgiveness but if we are building a proactive future for our marriage we want to protect it, care for it, and support each other to not have this storm make a repeat encounter in our lives. Our marriage needs to be filled with communicating with each other's weaknesses in mind, and not screaming at one another about our weaknesses.

Accountability in our weaknesses will help in building back trust. When we see a cop driving behind us on the highway, we naturally slow down. Their accountability reminds us that we aren't alone on the roads, that people are watching and checking in on us.

Building a proactive Marriage means more than getting through the storms of the past, it means protecting the foundation of your Marriage from future storms. The attacks on your marriage aren't done just because the rain from this storm season has ended. We have to care for our souls and take care of one another. We need to get to a place where we build a support network so that your spouse is not your only source of accountability. There may be a few people you need to pray about trusting to enter into this dark storm with you. You both have walked through something similar, and the right support can continue to disciple and care for you moving forward.

Spiritual Growth

Our faith journey should constantly be growing, this will be your utmost form of accountability, and having people to talk to about what God is showing, revealing, and teaching you is a necessity in growth. Please don't give me that "I am not a reader" speech. I bet you are the same person that says "I am not a prayer person". You need to read, you need to pray, you need to love, you need to hear, you need to listen. My husband isn't a "water" person, but you know what, he needs water. Sweet Tea and Coffee are good, but water is essential at refreshing and caring for the soul. In gaining accountability on your spiritual growth, find a way to keep yourself motivated on growing in your personal relationship with Christ. What can you be reading? Who can you be surrounding yourself around? How can you grow your prayer life?

Support

Find people that you can talk to about your struggles. An authentic community that you can be broken and beautiful in front of. These will be the people you won't want to lose hold of. If you don't have them, search for them. Don't wait for Halloween to come for them to knock on your door for some candy. Seek out the authentic community of believers, God-seekers, and humbly-broken friends that can walk alongside you.

Check-ins

Regularly checking in with your spouse will help you both stay connected and continue caring for each other. Your main focus with check-ins needs to be a focus on the heart of your spouse and not a fixation on behavior. Behavior and attitude is not a whole person, you need to check-in with their heart and mind. Be cautious of getting easily discouraged as you both learn to check-in with one another. You both need to understand that you process out loud differently, don't get frustrated when it doesn't pan out to look like the picture you had in your head. Instead, learn one another, see the differences in communication you both bring and find the value their style or personality adds to the relationship.

It can take a while to get a good flow going in a marital therapy room. There are three people in the room so finding peace, purpose, and clear direction for the sessions isn't a pretty picture in session one. It is a learned environment that is not natural. Check-ins with your spouse will be the same way, keep at them, learn about yourself and each other. Ask yourself how you both can make check-ins more of an encouraging and supportive conversation than a quarterly review of behavior and what's been accomplished. You are being proactive in developing a loving relationship, not continual meetings aimed at reminding your spouse of all they are that you dislike.

Comparisons

The last trap I don't want you to fall into as you look to have a proactive marriage is to make the goal for your marriage to look like someone else's marriage. It's just never going to happen. You will beat yourself up if you think every marriage has it together except yours.

We all have a story, you just know yours and only get to see parts of someone else's. The parts they want you to see.

The weather has been nice out, so we have been able to open the windows in our house to let in some fresh air. The problem is that we aren't used to that, so as our voices raise at our attempts to get our children to get ready for bed, put their shoes away, do their homework and so forth, we forget the windows are open. We will raise our voice at our kids, and then I will say to Matt, "the windows are open, the neighbors can hear us". Then Matt will yell up the stairs in a sweet and loud voice, "Oh dear sweet children, we would love it if you would come downstairs after you clean your room so we can eat dinner together as a family. I love you so much children." My husband is known for his sarcasm, and he continually makes me smile while I shake my head at him. Like the neighbors are going to believe that, that's not real either.

The point is that when we get stuck in the comparison trap with other couples, we are comparing to false realities, so it's a game you're never going to win. You both are striving to be the marriage and family that God has designed to the best of your ability on that day. You will mess up, you will get it wrong, BUT you will get it right, you will be amazing, you will love unconditionally, and you will apologize in your worst moments, but know you will have them. My hope as you get out of the comparison trap is that when you see a marriage or a family that doesn't have it altogether, you look at them and say, "I understand", or "it's ok". That you love the marriage and the family that is on their last breath trying to hold everything together. They need your support, and they need a meal, or a thoughtful card, a text or a phone call; not your judgment, and not your condemnation. We don't compare, we love. We love others even while knowing we don't have it together, and understanding they don't either. Just because you don't see someone's scars doesn't mean they don't have them.

Step VII
STEPPING OUTSIDE

The world feels different now. Almost like the universe shared a secret with you and you don't know how to talk about it with your friends. Step outside, it's time to take a look around.

Chapter 16
Reconciliation with Others

You have been working on getting your life right again before God and with your spouse. There is still more to be done, but now is a good time to go back to the list I had you make earlier on your path to acceptance where you needed to recognize all that your sin had impacted and the people you have hurt and begin to seek reconciliation with some of the people hurt by this storm. (No joke, most of you are going to read this section and skim right over it, or it is going to go in one ear and out the other because what I am asking you to do is face people.)

Now that you are making progress and you are gaining your strength from how God sees you over the way the world is looking and talking about you it is time to start facing them. When you truly believe in the identity that you are child of God, grasping on to His promises as He breathes into your lungs, and that He has transformed you through this, you will gain the strength to face the people that you wish you could run away from and avoid for the next couple of years.

Romans 12:18 needs to strike us as we hear the words "If it is possible, as far as it depends on you, live at peace with everyone."

There is a discovery we are making as we grow through the process of being redeemed, restored, and transformed, and the expectation we have is that everyone has been on the same journey with us. Disappointment sets in fast when we realize they haven't been. We may spend all day and night in the consummation of what to do and how to move on from this storm in our marriage, but everyone's life has moved on, everyone's world has continued to spin while yours felt like it stood completely still.

I am so glad that Paul put the line "If it is possible, as far as it depends on you...". He knew what I wish I didn't have to learn, that the peacemaker in me isn't going to find peace with everyone. I may long for it, I pray for it, but in reality, it isn't going to happen with everyone. That is a hard reality for this heart to sleep with at night. My desire for reconciliation is a bit extreme. I seem to take out that whole first part about "if it is possible" and only hear the ethical command to "live at peace with everyone". This is precisely what it means to look at scripture without its full context.

> *Journal: I need to do my part to be at peace with the people in my life that have been impacted by the hurt and disappointment I have caused. The trap I fall into is not getting the peace with everyone that the beautiful reconciling picture I have in my head has. I long for 'heaven on earth' moments when it comes to reconciliation. I see beautiful hugs on earth where people can see through pain and sin like our God does. My heart wishes for on earth what I know heaven will look like. I forget we aren't there yet.*

We have a biblical part to play in being at peace with others, but only a part. We can do things and show people our transformation to the best of our ability, but it will be God's transformation in their life that will determine what they do next. I told you at the beginning that every sin has a story, and every restoration has a story too, some of them will be good and some of them not so good. For some of you, the person you are seeking peace from is your spouse, and you made it to the end of this book alone, with them not wanting the peace from the relationship you desire in restoration. Their heart has been hardened, or they are unwilling to let go of the desires of their heart that swept them away, and your story is ending with sin pulling you apart. Or you weren't able to make it to the end together because your spouse is stuck unable to give forgiveness, unsure how to give it and probably struggling with something in their own life that keeps them from receiving it as well.

For others, the reconciliation you are hoping for is from the friends and family surrounding the storm. You and your spouse are gaining restoration together and are longing for the day when this is just the storm of '08, or whatever year yours was that just gets mentioned every once in a while. But the people who looked at you with disgust, who despised you and cursed your name through the battle, the people who don't sympathize with you, are the people you are wondering if you will ever be at peace with. The friendships you lost that you've been grieving over, and the future family gatherings that are going to get even more challenging to face.

Keep longing for peace. Peace is God's desire as well, but remember you are not in control of everything that happens next with the reconciliation of everyone this storm has touched. Your responsibility is in how you live and love to the best of your ability in obedience to God in the days to come, that is the focus moving forward.

Reconciliation can't be forced. If they aren't ready, we can't push our timing on their heart. God did a work in you, and now you need to believe that He can do a work in them too, but that doesn't mean it has to involve you (that one was hard for me to write, let's move on quickly).

Freedom in Christ

There are harsh truths that come during the process of being restored with those around you. Redemption and restoration are two different concepts I am learning in Christianity. We have freedom in Christ because He paid the penalty on our behalf for sin. Our redemption was bought with a price and thanks be to God that it has been paid. The freedom we have from the debt of falling into sin has already been redeemed; God did that for us through Christ, the controversial part among Christians is whether or not we are restored. Hopefully, as you have followed along in this process, you have seen the path of personal, spiritual, and marital restoration in our recovery of sin, but once we get to a place of feeling redeemed, some people may surround your life that will have trouble looking at you as restored.

Some people haven't watched you cry, haven't heard your pleas in the middle of the night for your Father to rescue you, people that haven't seen the weeks of turmoil and suffering you have just disparaged through. They see you emerged, and doing well, which in a lot of cases, means they feel safe enough now to say the hurtful things they didn't want to say up front. They have left you alone, and they have had months now to sit and stay up at night themselves, thinking through what they would say to you when they get the chance. Their disappointment has been festering while your healing has taken place.

These disappointed faces will be the ones you are turning to in working on reconciliation right now. Some of these voices are positive, and some are negative. You may finally feel a small glimmer of freedom, finally feeling God's voice from Isaiah 60 telling you to "rise". You rise and begin to feel the rays of sunlight again on your face, and as you step outside, you hear the voices of condemnation from others that have been hurt by you in the past. Their hurtful words and glares will blind-side you as you walk towards your spouse, family, and friends once more. The people that were hurt are still hurt unless they went through their own healing. If not, they may still be struggling to see a person beyond the sin.

Restoration and reconciliation seem to have a gray area as it means different things to different people, but being redeemed is confirmed, Christ did that for you. You may see some different opinions though, and some people even have a timeline for restoration where they don't believe you can be restored unless it is within the timetable they set for you. This becomes murky water for me as I see Jesus as a man who dissects the heart of his people. For me, a distinctive timeline for restoration is an earthly response to sin that seems to be present because we don't have the power of Christ to see into the heart of a person. If all we have are behaviors and patterns to look at, it seems our human tendency is to say we need a certain amount of time to pass before our belief in your restoration can be approved. Whether this is right or wrong, I am just letting you know how it is to prepare you and sit with you as we see this natural tendency unfold. I don't like it either, but it is out there.

Have you been listening to all the excruciatingly hard things I have already asked you to do? I am so proud of you, but we aren't done yet. We are all still intentionally working on things at home, and now it's time to step outside and see if we can gain reconciliation from the people this storm has touched. This process will be unique to your situation. As you are feeling freedom in Christ, remember that people you come across also feel like they have their own freedom, a freedom to say whatever they want about you. They can drop bombs and walk away and leave your sensitive skin to stew in it.

There is so much more for us to learn, but the biggest thing you need is hope. Don't lose sight of hope, even with the people you would think healing to be unimaginable. We started this book together searching for it, hearing hope as only a foreign word in our vocabulary, but now, on this page, my prayer for you, for your marriage, and for your life, is that you feel it. That hope and faith have become real and evident in your life. This journey is not over yet, and we will keep at it together. You are not alone; your marriage is not alone. And before you know it, someone else close to you is going to struggle through the recovery of sin in their marriage, and you are going to share your experiences with them because they are going to feel exactly the way you did on page one, that no one understands. You'll be there, to share your story, to describe the character of Christ you developed, and to walk the lonely rewarding path with them.

As you step out of isolation from this storm and begin to fully live again, know that some people will say words, or treat you in ways that will put you down, in ways that will beat you up, and in ways that will make you want to retreat into a dark corner. Please my friend, when words are said, persevere through those moments where people don't know how to love you. Remember that your life is not the label they give you. Be strong. Stay strong. Be courageous when the world tries to take away your dignity. Have faith in a God that is bigger than a bully in your life, even if that bully is in your family.

Chapter 17
Transformed in a New World

I remember when my sister was in middle school and she was getting her eyes checked after realizing how bad her vision was. My Mom felt awful for not being able to notice how bad my sister's vision had gotten. It's not like she was in pain, so she wasn't complaining about her sight. The world she saw around her was all she knew, and she didn't know what she was missing and didn't know that it could look any more detailed than the images she saw. When the eye doctor gave her the correct prescription her eyes needed, she stepped out of the doctor's office experiencing a new world. She would describe the common images that we take for granted and say, "I didn't realize that the trees had that much detail on them, I can see everything". It was as if she had become grateful and appreciative of an experience she never knew she was missing. The world hadn't changed, she just stepped outside with a new way of looking at it.

A similar thing has happened with the advancements in understanding the earth and the universe around us. There have been so many significant discoveries that have re-shaped our view of the world, and there are still many more things that are being researched and uncovered today. How neat is that? To learn that the world we have grown up learning about hasn't changed, just our understanding is what changes. As more scientific facts are brought to light, we learn more about the world we thought we knew everything about.

Science gives us a similar example of a perspective shift. There was a time when people's thinking was in agreement that the earth was flat and every bit of understanding about our world was only thought of through the context of the earth being flat. Before the insights of the astronomer, Galileo, people only had one stream of thought on their perspective of the world. After his published work in 1632 commenting on his beliefs of the earth being round, Galileo received push back and was considered a heretic for his theories. People pushed against the astronomer on the notion that it could be round, and it wasn't until after his death that people started hearing his theories with some weight. Once people believed something new, it changed everything. They had to think about things they never even questioned. Their perspective, their beliefs, and even their thoughts changed, and honestly, it's all because an astronomer was ok with trying out a new lens. We have a new lens, and our view of the earth is filtered through our beliefs of the earth being round or flat.

Perspective Shift

This perspective shift is where you are hopefully at on your marital journey through the storm, and you are seeing things with a different lens. What you believed about marriage on Day 1 or even on the first page of reading this book has shifted and changed as you have gone through the trial and benefit of learning how to love on the other side of sin. Your world may have felt shattered when we first began, but now you hopefully realize that it didn't fall apart, your marriage may have stayed intact, even if barely, but it was more turned upside-down than crushed into the pieces we initially saw on the floor.

We have been forced into a perspective shift where the person we once knew is still that person, just our image of them has shifted as we have gained new information into our discovery of their weaknesses and susceptibilities as well as our own. Hopefully, you have both learned more about each other through this process, learned how to care for your spouses' heart and the things in it they are most sensitive to. Hopefully, you have learned more about your Creator and the intensity of love He has for the both of you. Hopefully, you have found love for yourself beyond the voices of lingering shame. As I have encouraged you all along the way to this point, I will say to you again, we aren't done yet.

What Now?

I have found myself struggling to finish this book. The information I have given you is but a snapshot of all the truths, wisdom, knowledge, and understanding that is available. Each time I read through this on my computer I have something else to add and encourage you in. My husband and I have been continuously evolving as God hasn't stopped for a moment to teach us right now while He knows our ears are open. (Interesting how much you can learn if you just tell God you are listening.)

We have learned together that our marriage doesn't have to end when a storm hits, but that God can do something beautiful through the storm in our lives. We belong to a God that sent his Son for the hurting, for the ones that need to be redeemed, and the souls that feel broken. A God that shines a light on the dark places in our lives and can turn what the world uses to tear us down into something that strengthens us. Sin seeks destruction, but the recovery over sin has the power to tighten us together. To see a hurting spouse instead of a convicted one, allows us to care for each other at a deeper level than we ever had before. You may have begun your marriage only seeing a saint that you never thought would hurt you, and now you look past their smile and see their wounded heart and want to treasure, love, and care for them knowing you are loving one of God's children. These are but a few of the lessons we have learned on this journey.

I am not finished. God is not done teaching me and showing me, and He's not done with you either. This book does need to come to a close, but our growth in understanding shouldn't. Just as we can only adapt to the information we have about the earth around us, we can only function through the understanding we have of marriage at this moment. We have to be open to the fact that it could grow even more from this point on. The knowledge this experience has granted us does not extend to the fullness of what we can learn from marriage. We have more to come as God will continue and never cease to use our marriage, connection, and relationships with other people to teach us more about love, selflessness, character formation, and God's grace and glory than we will ever completely understand. At the beginning of this book I invited you to go on this journey, and in closing, I want to ask you not to stop the journey either. Commit to continue being molded. Allow your mind about relationships to be shifted, and your understanding of God's grand design be expounded through the discoveries you will have about what happens next.

Let's step out into the world together with a new lens realizing that the world hasn't changed as much as our understanding of it has. As one marriage at a time overcomes the storms that sin brings into our homes, we will regain the ability to bring light into the darkness, to bring hope to the hopeless situations, and bring life into areas the world would deem as dead. This is how we let the light of Jesus shine into the experiences of your family and mine.

RESOURCES

Chapter 2: Hope Hunt Exercise Examples

SONGS THAT HAVE INSPIRED US:

- *It is Well* Bethel Music and Kristene DiMarco, 2014
  - https://www.youtube.com/watch?v=YNqo4Un2uZI
- *Broken Things* Matthew West, 2017
  - https://www.youtube.com/watch?v=WdUu6ZsdVfM
- *Hills and Valleys* Tauren Wells, 2017
  - https://www.youtube.com/watch?v=p4rRCjrAyCs
- *Spirit of the Living God* Vertical Worship, 2015
  - https://www.youtube.com/watch?v=ogGOlGswStA
- *God of Miracles* Chris McClarney, 2015
  - https://www.youtube.com/watch?v=6m5oxG3_C5g
- *Nowhere* Sarah Reeves, 2017
  - https://www.youtube.com/watch?v=j7r0Ypu9dCs
- *You're Gonna Be Okay* Brian and Jenn Johnson, 2017
  - https://www.youtube.com/watch?v=LjF9IqvXDjY
- *Even If* Mercy Me, 2017
  - https://www.youtube.com/watch?v=B6fA35Ved-Y
- *I Wanna Go Back* David Dunn, 2016
  - https://www.youtube.com/watch?v=yUvxhGRUR3s
- *What a Beautiful Name* Hillsong, 2016
  - https://www.youtube.com/watch?v=nQWFzMvCfLE
- *Resurrecting* Elevation, 2016
  - https://www.youtube.com/watch?v=Rf8Zzn4nOzc
- *Forgiven* Crowder, 2016
  - https://www.youtube.com/watch?v=u_ZWEO36jok
- *Never Too Far Gone* Jordan Feliz, 2016
  - https://www.youtube.com/watch?v=TG6s8DxQJ5w
- *I Relent* Citizens and Saints, 2016
  - https://www.youtube.com/watch?v=c-klsnT_BTk

Chapter 2: Hope Hunt Exercise Examples

<u>SCRIPTURE VERSES (straight from my notecards):</u>

- There is no fear in love. But perfect love drives out fear, because fear has to do with punishment. The one who fears is not made perfect in love. 1 John 4:18

- In fact, this is love for God: to keep his commands. And his commands are not burdensome, for everyone born of God overcomes the world. This is the victory that has overcome the world, even our faith. 1 John 5:3,4

- You dear children, are from God and have overcome them, because the one who is in you is greater than the one who is in the world. 1 John 4:4

- See, I am doing a new thing! Now it springs up; do you not perceive it? I am making a way in the wilderness and streams in the wasteland. Isaiah 43:19

- He who was seated on the throne said, "I am making everything new!" Then he said, "Write this down, for these words are trustworthy and true. Revelation 21:5

- Fools mock at making amends for sin, but goodwill is found among the upright. Proverbs 14:9

- Whoever is patient has great understanding, but one who is quick-tempered displays folly. Proverbs 14:29

- Do everything without grumbling or arguing, so that you may become blameless and pure, "children of God without fault in a warped and crooked generation". Then you will shine among them like stars in the sky as you hold firmly to the word of life. And then I will be able to boast on the day of Christ that I did not run or labor in vain. Phillipians 2:14-16

- But he said to me, "my grace is sufficient for you, for my power is made perfect in weakness." Therefore I will boast all the more gladly about my weaknesses, so that Christ's power may rest on me. 2 Corinthians 12:9,10

- Before I was afflicted I went astray, but now I obey your word...It was good for me to be afflicted so that I might learn your decrees. Psalm 119:67,71
- Therefore, if anyone is in Christ, the new creation has come. The old has gone, the new has come. 2 Corinthians 5:17
- Indeed, there is no one on earth who is righteous, no one who does what is right and never sins. Ecclesiastes 7:20
- As you do not know the path of the wind, or how the body is formed in a mother's womb, so you cannot understand the work of God, the maker of all things. Ecclesiastes 11:5
- Before I formed you in the womb I knew you, before you were born I set you apart; I appointed you as a prophet to the nations. Jeremiah 1:5
- Therefore, there is no condemnation for those who are in Christ Jesus. Romans 8:1

Chapter 2: Hope Hunt Exercise Examples

IDENTIFY CHARACTER WORDS:

Accountable	Adaptable	Adventurous
Alert	Ambitious	Appropriate
Assertive	Astute	Attentive
Authentic	Aware	Bravery
Calm	Candid	Capable
Certain	Charismatic	Clear
Collaborative	Committed	Communicator
Compassion	Comradeship	Connected
Conscious	Considerate	Consistent
Contributes	Cooperative	Courageous
Creative	Curious	Dedicated
Determined	Diplomatic	Directive
Disciplined	Dynamic	Easygoing
Effective	Efficient	Empathetic
Empowers	Energetic	Enthusiastic
Ethical	Excited	Expressive
Facilitates	Fairness	Faithful
Fearless	Flexible	Friendly
Generative	Generosity	Gratitude
Happy	Hard Working	Honest
Honorable	Humorous	Imaginative
Immaculate	Independent	Initiates
Innovative	Inquiring	Inquiring

Integrates	Integrity	Intelligent
Intentional	Interested	Intimate
Joyful	Knowledgeable	Leading
Listener	Lively	Logical
Loving	Loyal	Manages Time Well
Networker	Nurturing	Open-Minded
Optimism	Organized	Patient
Peaceful	Planner	Playful
Poised	Polite	Powerful
Practical	Presents Self Well	Proactive
Problem-Solver	Productive	Punctual
Reliable	Resourceful	Responsible
Self-confident	Self-generating	Self-reliant
Sense of Humor	Sensual	Serves Others
Sincere	Skillful	Spiritual
Spontaneous	Stable	Strong
Successful	Supportive	Tactful
Trusting	Trustworthy	Truthful
Versatile	Vibrant	Warm
Willing		

Chapter 5: Road to Recovery

Exercise: Road Blocks *Example*

	ROAD BLOCK	BREAK THROUGH TACTIC
(1) Seek out counsel (Gain wise advice)	*Financial – I just don't know how I am going to afford seeing a Counselor right now.*	*I will start by exploring the options in my area and see if I can find a resource that can help me, or offer a sliding scale for services.*
(2) Work on Unraveling the details (with safety)	*I don't even know where to start, I don't feel safe talking to anybody right now.*	*I can start by journaling what I am able to say right now, I can start with writing things that I am having trouble saying about my life.*
(3) Understand sin and suffering believing there is healing on the horizon.	*I can't even begin to believe in healing right now! I am so consumed with hatred and anger.*	*I can begin to see what God sees when He looks at a world filled with disobedience and sin. I can look in God's word and hold onto the promises that are hard to believe right now in my life.*

CHAPTER 6: Marital Damage Assessment Exercise

Today, we will focus on today. Each of you take some time to fill in the blanks of your observations right now. If you have trouble starting here, do this exercise on a separate piece of paper to get you started. As you answer these three questions, answer them as best you are able to right now, even if you have to leave things blank or if you end up writing too much. After some time passes, do this exercise again and notice how your ability to make assessments will develop as your level of awareness and clarity increases.

1. What's Been Done?

HIS OBSERVATIONS	HER OBSERVATIONS

2. What Needs to be Done?

HIS OBSERVATIONS	HER OBSERVATIONS

3. Prioritize the Needs

HIS OBSERVATIONS	HER OBSERVATIONS

Chapter 7: Name it Exercise

A great way to examine if you are in a place of Shock and Denial right now is to see what you are able to name and claim. This is a way of going further into your Marital Damage Assessment Form.

1. Are there any more parts of the storm you may be ready to own as you move out of Shock and Denial?

2. Are there any new observations of what needs to be done or even new prioritizations as you begin to see out of the fog?

Chapter 8: Checklist for turning back to God (James 4:7-10)

As you sit in confusion not knowing what to do next, and scrolling the internet for self-help tips for your life, God gives us the steps we need. James lines it out for us in this scripture, but for all my checklist readers out there (which I am one of), let me put James 4:7-10 into a step-by-step list to help us with clear direction:

1. Submit yourselves back to God.
2. Turn away from the friendship we made with the devil and the earthly flesh within our sin.
3. Seek out God. Read, fast, pray. Take action steps to get closer to him and He will come near to you.
4. Now that you have God near you, you have His strength with you to help you get clean, to purify your heart and your mind.
5. Grieve, mourn, and wail. As you gain a cleansed spirit, you will grieve as you fully start to grasp your disobedience and His faithful love.
6. You will go through a season where your happiness and joy are turned to mourning and gloom in your sadness and recovery.
7. In doing these things you will become stripped, and through the stripping process you will be humbling yourself before the Lord, but He has a plan to lift you up.

Sited References

Adler, A. *The Individual Psychology of Alfred Adler.* New York: Basic Books, 1956

Association, A. P. *Diagnostic and Statistical Manual of Mental Disorders 5th ed.* Arlington, VA: Author, 2013.

Beck, A. *Love is never enough: How couples can overcome misunderstandings, resolve conflicts, and solve relationship problems through cognitive therapy.* New York: Harper and Row, 1988.

Bruckheimer, J. (Producer), & Verbinski, G. (Director). *Pirates of the Carribbean: The curse of the Black Pearl* [Motion Picture]. United States, 2003.

Cloud, H & Townsend. *Boundaries in Marriage: Understanding the choices that make or break loving relationships.* Grand Rapids, MI: Zondervan, 1999.

Eliot, G. *Daniel Deronda.* New York: Modern Library, 2002.

Gottman, J. M., & Silver, N. *The seven principles for making marriage work: A practical guide from the country's foremost relationship expert.* New York: Three Rivers Press, 1999.

Keller, T. *The Meaning of Marriage: Facing the complexities of commitment with the wisdom of God.* New York: Penguin Books, 2011.

Kuligan, V. *Ten things I wish Jesus never said*. Wheaton, IL: Crossway Books, 2006.

Lewis, C. *The Problem of Pain*. New York: HarperCollins Publishers, 1940.

Manning, B. *The Ragamuffin Gospel*. Colorado Springs: Multnomah Books, 1990.

Meyer, J. *Approval Addiction*. New York: Faith Words, 2005.

Smalley, G. *Fight your way to a better marriage*. New York: Howards Books, 2012.

Thomas, G. *Sacred Marriage: What if God designed marriage to make us holy more than to make us happy*. Grand Rapids: Zondervan, 2000.

Wallard, D. *The Divine Conspiracy: Recovering our hidden life in God*. New York: Harper, 1998.

About the Author

Emily Funderburk graduated from Gordon-Conwell Theological Seminary with a master's degree in counseling, and she is currently a licensed professional counselor in North Carolina; she brings a unique blend of ministry experience and counseling practice to her writings on the impact that emotional and spiritual health has on our marriages. Emily is the mother of three children, and she and her husband of thirteen years, Matt, have learned the value and definition of love and forgiveness through the storms and celebrations in their life together.

Printed in the United States
By Bookmasters